Navigations

*One man explores
the Americas
and discovers himself*

Ted Kerasote

Stackpole Books

Copyright © 1986 by Ted Kerasote

Published by
STACKPOLE BOOKS
Cameron and Kelker Streets
P.O. Box 1831
Harrisburg, PA 17105

In slightly altered forms, these pieces have been contributed to the following
magazines:

"Flying For 1002"	*Alaska*
"Alder"	*Audubon*
"Water Dreams In The Desert"	
"A Trophy Line"	*Cross-Country Skier*
"Entelechy"	*Mountain Gazette*
"A Record Snook"	*Sports Afield*
"Sign Of The Fishes"	
"Baja"	
"Neva Hurry"	

Printed in the U.S.A.

Library of Congress Cataloging-in-Publication Data

Kerasote, Ted.
    Navigations: one man explores the Americas and
discovers himself.

    1. America – Description and travel – 1981–
2. Kerasote, Ted – Journeys – America.   I. Title.
E27.5.K47   1986   917.3'0492   86-5723
ISBN 0-8117-1013-0

for Elpis,
for George,
who give all

and for Comi
who danced
who ran
who beat the gong each day

Contents

8

Home

Introduction

The man who finds his homeland sweet is still a tender beginner; he to whom every soil is as his native one is already strong; but he is perfect for whom the entire world is a constantly new and foreign land.

after Hugo of St. Victor,
a 12th Century Saxon monk

Orienting The Map

In his hut above the Rio Bayano, deep in the Darien rain forest of Panama, the Cuna Indian chief sat. His cheeks glowed with henna, his black hair was cut off straight at his shoulders, his chest was bare. He wore a seedy gray fedora and smoked a Marlboro and was stupendously drunk on chica, a brew his tribe made from corn and downed on fiesta days until the whole village was singing and dancing.

The chief, sipping from the mug by his side, was being as lucid as one could expect and more than hospitable under the circumstances, these being that I had appeared out of the jungle carrying a large backpack, announced that I was hiking to Colombia (quite a ways off), and asked to hire a guide, since my maps were blank from this point on. In addition, it being the rainy season (rain poured off my bare head), the trails were washed out, and I was having a hell of a time making out where I should be going, not to mention where I was.

The group of drunk young men who listened to this speech at the river bank said it was a shame indeed that I had come in the rainy season (I had to agree), and that I had a long way to go to Colombia (no doubt), and that they'd take me up to see the chief (now we're getting somewhere), but not to expect a guide for days, maybe even a week, for, you see (they smiled drunkenly), it was the fiesta of the chica!

The chief, a short handsome man who, in the U.S., would have made a terrific Congressman, agreed sadly with everything his boys had told me. And sweeping his arm across his large hut – reed walls, thatched roof, dirt floor – said, "Hang your hammock anywhere. *Mi casa es su casa.*" My house is your house.

It was. For days. Until I said, "Hey, amigo, rainy season or no, chica or no (I'd had plenty), I got to get going. You see, winter's almost over in South America, and I have this date with some Chilean powder . . . no, not cocaine, snow, *nieve.*" I did a little wedel, so he would get the idea.

"Ah-ha!" exclaimed the chief, leering. *"Una mujer!"* A woman.

Well, who was it that said skiing the steep and deep was like making love? And so I took out my map, and the chief and I sat down on his log threshold above the river, and he said, his stubby brown finger moving over the map, "You go up the Rio Nargandi and over this long hill and down the Rio Chucunaque until you get to Yaviza. And that's a ten day trip. Then you go up the Rio Paya."

Concentrating with my full attention (after all there were banditos out there, and jaguars, and fer de lances, a snake from whose bite one never returned), I followed his finger for a while, until I noticed that he held the map upside down and his finger, instead of tracing my proposed route, was taking me back toward Costa Rica.

I sighed, and cleared my throat, and said, "That way up the river?" I pointed to the actual river before us.

"Si, si, exactamente!" the chief cried and also pointed up the river. As he let go of the map, I turned it around on his knees.

"And when you get to the Atrato Swamp . . ." Looking down, he stabbed his finger on the map. ". . . go straight into the rising sun." At this point his finger sailed off Panama and into the Carribean, setting me on a course for Cuba.

The good chief and the entire village sent me on my way with waves, a coconut, a stem of plaintain, and two bottles of chica. I wandered around the jungle for another week and never got to Colombia, at least not overland. I blamed the rainy season, the washed out trails, the flooded rivers, but most of all those bloody maps with their blank spaces – no contour lines, no shaded relief, the villages not even on the right bends of the rivers. I didn't realize that it would take me ten more years to read maps well. In fact, I had no idea that I was navigating in country for which a good map had not yet been made.

Funny . . . today the Cuna chief with his five children and happy wife is on my mind – this fall day in Eldorado Canyon, as I sit atop a pinnacle of rock and see, to the east, the Great Plains, holding farms and Denver. To the west are pine-covered hills, connecting this transition zone of uplifted sandstone to the big snow peaks of the Rockies. Cosmopolites, ranchers, mountaineers, oilmen – the Front Range of Colorado has held them all. Despite its bad air and congestion, I've liked the place. It tries to be something to everyone and occasionally, like today, can be a high enough viewpoint from which to take a bearing.

The sky is a calm, innocent blue and its curve – dipping over the edges of the plains toward the Gulf of Mexico and bending in the opposite direction over the Rockies – is palpable, as if a coverlet had been unfurled above the planet and tucked around the horizons.

Once, soon after hiking through the Darien Jungle, I said I was going to get back to my Cuna chief. Get a kayak, go down the Chucunaque, across the Atrato, see those gators. Never did. Too many other trips were conceived along the way, like unexpected children who need care and love, until the first trips, and the dreams they birthed, have become like a career I put aside for a second one, a third, this endless spume wake trailing from a ship and disappearing into the sea.

Naturally, I've been accused of having a bad case of wanderlust. I've also been told that I'm incapable of dealing with the risks of stability. The latter stab, coming from someone I loved, left me guilt-ridden for a time, until I actually left this hemisphere and discovered that I loved other continents as much as North and South America, that, in fact, I am one of those strange people who is in love with navigating itself – with the act of finding and re-finding the way, and not forgetting any of the paths which have brought me to my present camp. Perhaps nomads – those roamers of the steppes and tundra – are some of the happiest people because of their relation to shelter. Since almost anyplace is home, they need never arrive. Feeling comfortable nearly everywhere, they are rarely lost.

Though the southwestering sun is warm on my face, my back is cold. I remember that the year is growing dark up on the Peace River in Alberta and in Denali the bears are denning. But on the opposite Pole, in Patagonia, the brant are building nests. If I close my eyes, it's easy to feel it all – the curve of the planet beneath me, green and blue without political boundaries to interrupt the crescents of the mountains and the arcs of the rivers. When I can't return to a place, this is a way to pay a visit, while also seeing what lies ahead.

Unfortunately, both views are short. The evening will fall. I'll move on, and with two feet back on the ground, it is sometimes difficult to remember exactly what I have seen from above. That's okay. I've learned that if I rely on maps, even those I've made myself, I eventually reach a place where they join inexactly – where the contour lines don't meet, the compass makes no sense, where there's not even a high viewpoint from which to take a bearing. Then there's nothing to do except put them away and navigate by the feel of the country.

The author fishing in Central America. Photo by James Billipp.

South

Whenever it is a damp, drizzly November in my soul . . . I account it high time to get to sea as soon as I can.

Herman Melville

A Record Snook

Today was the seventh day I've tried to catch a record snook, here on the north coast of Costa Rica. I don't remember all that's happened in the past week. It has been mostly hot and sunny, the surf high and white. I've risen each dawn and have eaten only papaya and pineapple before hurrying my guide to the boat. Racing through the lagoons, we've alarmed the cranes and amused the toucans, and I've been casting as the sun has risen and the other fishermen have been drinking their coffee back in camp. One day it rained.

This morning the sky was a pleasant, thought-provoking blue, and I foolishly began to hope that the largest snook ever caught on this meager tackle was still twenty pounds and that some other fisherman, who had also tired of the usual sport of dragging fish from the sea and had begun to divert himself in this eccentric way, hadn't caught a record snook and submitted proof of its capture to the International Game Fish Association.

For many anglers the I.G.F.A. has become nothing more than a group of persnickety old men who try to regulate what was once a happy-go-lucky sport. Nonetheless, if you throw your hat into the ring, you can't ignore those who keep the rules. Like Olympic committees and dictionary editors, the I.G.F.A. performs an invaluable service: it helps to maintain the standards of our culture, its particular function being to verify the capture of our great fish.

It does this for the largest individual fish of each species as well as for the heaviest one taken in each line class. There are seven of these classes, ranging from six to one hundred thirty pounds, and many rules governing the proper matching of rods to reels to lines and how a fish must be played in order to be termed "A Record." It is a tedious and soul-wearying task, this verification, but to some men gives great pleasure.

On the first day that I became a participant in the I.G.F.A.'s game, I had a chance to reflect upon the worth of its rules. Bill Barnes, the owner of Casa Mar, the fishing camp where I'm staying, had joined me in the late afternoon and had waded into the surf next to me; although I had cast to the slough before us many times, his first cast produced a twenty-seven-pound snook.

Events – the rigging of tackle, an angler casting in a certain direction, a fish swimming along the breakers and sighting a lure he believes to be a tasty morsel – are permuted by an inscrutable law. On Bill's tackle the snook became our dinner. On my rod it would have been "The New World Record." Happiness or death may strike us by the way in which our face is turned.

Bill, busy with the running of the camp, was unable to join me during the following days. I continued alone and on the third morning, the rainy one, hooked and landed a twelve-pound snook, or *robalo*, as the Central Americans say. From his backbone I took the most tender meat and made *ceviche*, the wonderful hors d'oeuvre of this tropic land. Seated on the veranda of the lodge, the other fishermen and I ate our *ceviche*, drank rum, and talked merrily of the day's sport. I wondered, though, as I saw the eyes of the night birds begin to glisten in the voicing trees, where the lights of fish and men's eyes go when, from the edge of their universe, the will of some fisherman extinguishes them.

In the drowsy moments of the afternoon, when the waves have crawled in slow measure along the coast, I've watched the squadrons of pelican dip over the breakers and the soaring Vs of the frigate birds. While I've cast, the undertow has sucked me into the sea and the waves have pushed me back–over and over, three-quarter time.

During the space of two hundred waves I've sung every song I know: Arlo Guthrie and Gordon Lightfoot songs, Pete Seeger and Beatle songs, and folk songs too old to remember who sang them first. I've recited poetry: Robert Frost and Robert Browning; Shakespeare, Wyatt and Blake; Masefield, Eliot and more. Smiling big sun smiles, open teeth, laughing spring smiles into the sky, I've listened to my voice roll out among the waves. Sometimes I've taken half-an-hour to run three miles up the beach and have felt clear-headed and strong-lunged after it.

Six days went by.

Today a snook, eager to eat my jig, swam out of a receding wave and was nearly stranded upon the sand. He missed the lure. Shortly thereafter a fish struck viciously and was immediately gone. It was late afternoon and the sky had become slate gray. Along the horizon cannonballs of silver rolled into the sea.

On the beach with me was a commercial fisherman from the village of Bara Colorado. He hooked and lost a snook on his heavy spinning outfit. Then nothing except the slowness of the waves and the malingering clouds. Ominously they began to blanket the sky.

I jogged up the coast and when I returned, the commercial fisherman, bare-chested and up to his waist in the surf, was fighting another fish. Not a kilometer up the beach I had seen a tiger shark hunting and I warned the fisherman, who came closer to the land.

While he fought his snook I rigged a white jig and began to send long casts over the breakers. Behind me I heard Juan, my guide, yell, "It's five-thirty." Back in the Rio Colorado, where we had beached the boat, he had been sleeping away the afternoon.

The fisherman landed his fifteen-pound snook and began to walk toward the boats with Juan. I continued to fish; they yelled and gestured for me to come along. The entire sky was covered with storm clouds, the river was choppy, and dinner was probably on the table. But I had promised myself five more casts. I was on the third when a fish plucked the lure from the spume. I reared back and he was solid. I raised my rod for Juan to see. He and the fisherman stopped.

The snook began to swim along the beach, a tactic surf-fish often employ and which the angler can counter by walking abreast of his quarry. However I soon met an obstruction: a tossed-up jam of trees where the Rio Colorado joined the sea. The snook's course was going to take my line around this obstacle. For a few seconds the fish hesitated between the sea and the river; then he decided to swim into the Colorado instead of toward the open ocean. I was forced to follow him around the jam, up to my thighs in the waves. And although I stayed close to the logs I didn't care for it, after all there were the sharks; but there was nothing else to be done.

Then I saw a tree that completely blocked my way. Its roots were ten feet in the air and plunged like a frightened horse. For a moment I thought, hoped, that the snook might change his heading. But, of course, he chose to go around the tree. My line began to approach the roots where it would instantly part.

I didn't want to go any deeper into the surf, so I climbed onto the trunk, at the same time extending my rod around the tangle of roots. I tried to grab it from the other side— no luck. Suddenly the tree bucked, and I was thrown into the waves.

I held my breath, swam beneath the roots, and emerged on the far side. I stumbled out of the breakers, and Juan was right there, yelling at me that a *muchacha* had been taken by a *tiburon*, a shark, at this very spot, and I was *loco, absolutomente loco!* I had thought about the sharks and what I had done was crazy— but it's not often that you hook a record snook.

Obstinately the fish began to run toward the far bank of the river. Without hesitating, he took two hundred yards of line. The commercial fisherman had walked down the beach and stood by my side. His face was lit by a deep appreciation of what was happening. "It is a very great *robalo*," he said.

The very great *robalo* angled back toward the ocean, swam a huge arc beyond the curling breakers, and took the line around the tree once again.

The commercial fisherman and I walked toward the tree—its roots faced us like the head of Medusa. The fisherman said,

"Climb over to the other side, and I'll hand your rod around the front."

We were up to our waists in the roiled swells, the evening was upon us, and I thought, one of those lucid flashes: if he touches the rod, the record is disqualified. It is a rule of the I.G.F.A. – no one but the angler may touch the tackle while the fight is in progress. Who will ever know what happened on this Costa Rican beach? Who?

"No," I shouted over the noise of the surf. I started around the front of the tree.

"I'll protect you then." He swam into the sea before me.

A breaker crashed over us; passed. I leapt up and saw his face reappear, laughing.

"*Hombre!*" I gasped.

"*Que locura!*" he yelled. What madness.

And we managed to get out of the surf.

I walked along the beach. The snook paused. I thought I was gaining; then he began a run toward Africa. I could feel his strength through the rod, and I didn't know which was more powerful: the fish or the thought of capturing him. There logs and shrubs floating down the river, and the storm waves threw them into the air. My line was heavy with weed, stretched across the flotsam, ready to break. Yet it held and sang in the wind. What a thing of pride it would be to catch this fish! I pleaded with the river, "Please stop flowing;" implored the trees, "Go back to land;" told the snook, "Stop running." And they rushed out to sea with my hopes.

I felt a scrape, a pull. The line was loose, not completely. It dragged the weight of the lure.

"Reel! Reel!" the fisherman cried, cranking his hand in the air. The rod was bent with the weight of the very distant line and some seaweed. He believed that it was the fish, running toward the beach. I could actually feel my chest collapse in disappointment, and, after a minute of reeling, I brought in a forlorn piece of brown kelp.

The fisherman and Juan were standing around me. It was almost night, a red patch hung over the jungle palms; mutely we looked at the sand. They shook their heads – how many steaks that *robalo* would have made! And since they now fish with spinning rods instead of spears – what a fish it would have been to take on line so thin! *"Demasiado delgado!"* Too thin! Juan repeated, rubbing the chaffed line through his fingers. And the fisherman who had swum through the surf with me said, "Surely the snook would have been *el récord."*

I hooked the jig into one of the rod guides. "Tomorrow morning," Juan comforted. Carrying my tackle box, he began to run toward the boat. He was late for dinner.

We followed him and, as we walked over the sand, I thought about changing to a plug with small treble hooks that might not pull so easily. The single hook of the jig, no matter how finely honed, was too large to set with six-pound test line. The commercial fisherman departed in his dugout and we pushed our skiff into the river. I sat on the middle thwart as we bounced over the chop. Lights were on in the shacks along the shore, and Bill would be standing on the dock with Sr. Ronaldo, the head boatman, and Juan's father. They would be worrying – perhaps we had become greedy and had gone out to sea for tarpon.

As we motored through the lagoons, I thought about changing my spinning reel to a conventional model. They ususally had smoother drags and didn't give surges of slack that the fish could use to throw the hook. I also thought of switching to a slightly stiffer rod. And, as I mulled, I began to imagine the fish I had lost, stretching across the bottom of the skiff from gunwale to gunwale. I remembered the flimsiness of the line, the powerless rod, the puny reel, and I smiled sarcastically. A *robalo grande* simply couldn't be caught with these fragile tools . . . or perhaps I wasn't yet skillful enough in their use.

When we arrived at camp, a thirty-two pound snook was lying on the dock. The lucky fisherman had caught the grand fish on the other side of the river, not a kilometer from where I had been fishing. Using flashbulbs, he took many pictures of him, and other fishermen, who had caught only small lagoon fish during their stay at Casa Mar, crouched next to the snook and had themselves photographed alongside him.

Displaying a wild sleek motion even in death, the meter-long snook, a single black stripe down his flank, shone with the texture of wet marble. It was marvelous to behold him there on the planks of the dock; to touch him; to know that he had swum in the surf so close to us all; that he might have been ours. However, on the twenty-pound line which the fisherman had used, the snook was not even close to being cited "A Record."

First Mountain

It's twenty-four miles into the valley of Aconcagua, twenty-four miles of tundra, boulders, and talus, along a stream swollen with glacial milk. Sand clings underfoot, wind blasts from the surrounding peaks. Everywhere is the clean, sharp smell of stone. We carry 80-pound loads and walk bent over like humble pilgrims. In one long day and part of the next cold morning, we reach a large cabin at the base of our mountain. When we swing open the door, it's cold as a tomb inside, the wood floor ringing hollowly under our boots. The stacks of canned food and the bottles of gasoline left by descending climbers seem a memento to the dead who have perished above rather than support for those who will follow. While Bill and Steve sort through the stores, I walk back outside, stand on the steps, still in the morning shadow of the great peak, and look up. The summit is nearly two vertical miles above, a tan and stupendously barren precipice lit gold by the sun. This bit of crumbling volcanic stone is the highest point in the Western Hemisphere, the lookout of the cordillera that stretches from the Arctic Ocean to Cape Horn at the tip of South America. Three months ago I didn't know it's name: Aconcagua. Say it again, Aconcagua. Now I want to stand atop it, putting my five-odd feet above its 22,956 foot bulk. I have never done anything like this before. I have never even had the desire. But then I've never known two men like Bill and Steve.

"Hey, give us a hand!" Their shout comes from the cabin. I wrench my eyes from the summit where, the Argentine officials have told us, a dead Japanese climber sits, a smile frozen on his face.

We stow some extra food in our packs and make up a cache of fuel, for which one of us will return tomorrow. Shouldering the unwieldy loads we start up the steep switchbacks that climb through the broken rock of a buttress and disappear onto a plateau at 14,000 feet. Above are glaciers.

Bill walks first, I second, Steve last, miming how we met. . . . I had come to Otovalo, Ecuador to see a colorful wool market, held weekly. Indians in fedoras and ponchos hawked blankets and shirts while tourists from America and Europe strolled by the stalls. In the center of the square a group of photographers pushed at each other, vying for the best angles, and called to the Indians for poses.

A slight blond man in blue sailor pants appeared next to me. He wore a wispy beard and gently stroked a pile of blankets. His companion, a large woman with braids, looked at the photographers and said, "Why this reminds me of the Assyrian horde in that poem by . . . by . . . who wrote that?"

The blond man shrugged. I looked up, let a moment pass, then said, "Byron."

"Why yes," she said. "Do you know how it ends?"

I did and quoted her the lines, which finished, "And the might of the gentile unsmote by the sword/Hath vanished like snow in the glance of the Lord."

"Perfect," said her companion.

The facts of our being in this famous wool market in the unlikely spot of Otovalo, Ecuador were exchanged quickly. Bill Liske and Susan Kinne, two instructors for a Colorado-based wilderness school called Outward Bound, were in Ecuador trying to climb Chimborazo, the country's highest mountain and one made famous by the nearly complete first ascent of the scientist-

explorer Alexander von Humboldt. They had failed on the mountain and were now sightseeing. A third member of their party,
Steve Andrews, had stayed in Quito, recovering from a cold. I
offered that I had been traveling for 11 months through Central
America, fishing and exploring along the way, and was now
hoping to do some trout fishing in a high lake nearby.

"Do you have a fly rod?" asked Bill.

"Two," I said.

"I never learned," he mentioned.

"I could show you."

Susan drifted off and I think two hours passed as we talked of
flyrods, shotguns, Tintern Abbey, Voltaire, BMW motorcycles,
and a mountain above Aspen, Colorado.

He decided to go fishing; Susan caught a bus back to Quito. We
spent the weekend in a stone hut on a deserted island, roasting
potatoes on the fire and casting to trout who rose to the flies but
didn't bite. It didn't matter. If either of us had been a woman,
we'd have been lovers.

On Monday we took the afternoon bus to Quito. In their small
but fashionable hotel, I met Steve Andrews. Too tall for the low
whitewashed ceilings, his nose red from cold and sunburn, he
engulfed my hand. Dangling from the open closet doors and
stacked in the corners of the room were purple ropes, harnesses,
tattered packs, ice axes, pickets, screws, boots, sooty stoves, and
the blooming folds of an orange tent. At the time I didn't know
what half the gear was. I did know, however, that it was the stuff
people used to climb mountains.

I took a room down the street from them. Within two days Bill
and Susan left for Peru. Steve and I stayed on in Quito, he expecting a camera, which his Dad was sending from California to
replace one that had been stolen in Colombia, I awaiting a check
from a magazine. We explored opposite parts of the city, taking
breakfast and sometimes dinner together. Over meals he told me
about the school for which Bill, Susan, and he worked – Outward
Bound. "You know," he said, "when a ship leaves port and sails off
on its own." Founded by Kurt Hahn, a German educator who had
fled Hitler's Reich in the Thirties, O.B., as Steve called it, was
born out of the need to train British seamen to survive in the
North Atlantic after being torpedoed. Successful at that wartime

job, it became a public institution in the Fifties, training young English, Scot, and Welsh boys not only in ocean sailing but in hiking, mountaineering, and kayaking. The school's central idea – sound body, sound mind – was carried to the Continent and to the United States where, high in the mountains of Colorado, by the old mining town of Marble, the first ropes course and cabins were built in 1963. Steve had been a student of the fifth course and was now an instructor – one of those . . . "admirable" was the word that came to mind . . . admirable young men and women who spent half their year leading younger men and women around the tundra and forest of the Rockies only to take their accumulated paychecks and set off to see Africa, Nepal . . . South America. Steve had done even more traveling: he had lived through a 13-month tour of combat duty in Vietnam.

We were in a restaurant, eating chicken and rice at a table set with blue oilcloth, when he offered this bit of information. Nixon was in the midst of Watergate, and Steve, like Bill and me, had gone to college when the tear gas had been flying. When I asked him why he had gone to Southeast Asia, not only had gone but volunteered, he shrugged and mentioned that he didn't want to be drafted. He took a mouthful of rice and chewed it about twice as long as he usually chewed his food, which was a long time indeed. When he finished he said, "Actually, I wanted to see what a war was about."

We hike up toward the cold blue sky, one switchback, two, eight, twelve. Andrews takes one lanky, measured step after another. It's two miles to the top, he's reminded us. Go fast and you'll die. Bill, using the dash and collapse theory, pushes on ahead. Torn between my two mentors, I try to keep up with Bill but soon begin to pant. I fall back to Steve.

As he and I had left Quito in the dawn, heading south to meet Bill and Susan in Lima, we had seen Cotapaxi, a dreamy, Fugi-like peak, rising above the roofs and palm trees.

"You know," said Andrews, looking up at Cotapaxi's white slopes, "I'd like to climb a big mountain before going home."

The bus bumped over a rough section of road, and Steve's face became thoughtful. "Maybe Aconcagua. It's the biggest peak in South America, North America too."

About a mile down the road, I said, "Let's do it."

At dusk we pitch our tent at the edge of the small plateau called Plaza Mulas. Sharing the basecamp are a group of Austrians and a dozen Italians. To our right, on the very edge of the precipice, is a log *refugio*, guyed to the buttress with cable. Downvalley the sky turns a soft lavender, while above us a sprawling cirque catches the last pink light on its glaciers. The summit of Aconcagua, as always, is the last to give up the rays of the sun. We stand, hands in the pockets of our down parkas, and gaze to its saffron-colored pinnacle, now 9000 feet away.

In Bolivia I had bought an ice ax. In Chile a parka and windpants. In Argentina boots. We climbed a small peak where Bill and Steve demonstrated how to arrest a fall with the ax by leaping down a slope, turning on their stomachs, and plunging the pick of the ax into a hard snow. They asked me to do the same. I did it twice and they said, "You're ready." Susan, on the other hand, decided to go home.

Alpenglow now lights the peak and the wind like a predatory animal rips at the tent and is gone. We crawl into our bags before the stars appear. Bill mutters something that sounds like "oh." The tent rattles in the wind, *then the wind quiets and I'm walking the fields with my grandfather. We're carrying hundred-pound bags of manure, and my grandfather smells of sheep and fertile ground. The sweat drips off his brown face and arms. We throw down our bags, they split open and tomatoes spring out of the earth. We fetch another two bags, throw them on the next plowed row, and melons appear. "One more," he says. Fields of corn spring from our bags and stretch as far as we can see.*

My grandfather and I walk slowly and happily through the corn. In each ripe ear is a girl's head, a girl with sheaves for hair and an Indiana sky for eyes. He grabs an ear, pries it from the stalk, and offers it to me. I reach out my hand.

He pulls back the ear, a sly look in his old brown eyes. The girl's hair droops through his fingers.

I know what he wants. "Find someone else," I say. "Ask P.V."

I turn and walk away. At the edge of the road, I hear footsteps coming through the corn after me. Scared, I turn to meet him.

His face is no longer baiting. The lines around his mouth are filled with dust and disappointment. Slowly, full of regret, he hands me the ear. But when I reach out my hand to take it, he and the girl fade away.

Someone has poured sand in my eyes and my head aches. Steve and Bill are burrowed deep in their bags, not even a nose exposed. I struggle into my boots (neither of my friends moves), start the stove, and put on the pot of water which we collected from a bit of runoff last night. The pot is frozen solid and pings as the flames lick up its sides. The cracking of the ice rouses Steve. He and I cook some oatmeal and take it into the tent to Bill, who emerges from his bag looking like a man who has a hangover, the flu, and a broken neck all at the same time. We drink the pot of tea, brew another, pack the rucksacks with food, and shortly before nine, moaning and grumbling, head toward the glacier.

We're bound for 17,000 feet where there's another small, flat spot and a tiny hut called Antardica Argentina. Our plan is to cache food there, return to Plaza Mulas for a rest day, then occupy the 17,000-foot camp. The following day, if all goes well, we'll carry food to 20 and return to 17. Then we'll spend a night at 20 and on the next day make a dash for the summit at nearly 23,000 feet. This system of climbing high and sleeping low is supposed to acclimatize the body to altitude. It all seems so scientific as Steve explains it to me in the tent.

But as we kick steps in the hard snow of the *nieve penitentes,* 20-foot-high columns of ice packed closely together, and the way turns up into the huge scree slope known as the Gran Acarreo, the equation doesn't balance. In the loose pebbles we make one actual step of upward progress for every two steps we take. My headache, which had receded to a dull throb after breakfast, feels as if a blacksmith is driving a spike into my brain. There's no air going into my lungs even though I'm taking three breaths every step. I can hear the stones crunch under my boots; my stomach sours; I want to puke. The need to throw up is so overpowering that I actually get down on one knee and begin to wretch. Thinking of my two friends seeing me in this condition forces me to swallow my breakfast. Steve hands me a bottle of water and an orange. We snack, go on. I try to repeat the stages of our plan – carry to 17,000 feet, rest at 14 . . . but our neat progress disappears into the glistening drops that pulse in front of my eyes. When we reach a level section, I look down and notice, with a strange and euphoric joy, that the world has turned into a jagged skyline of purple and gray spires, all below us, as if seen from an airplane. When the trail steepens again my head throbs loud enough to hear. Who am I to be climbing the biggest mountain in the Western Hemisphere? Why am I doing this? Questions seem to stick on the dry roof of my mouth before I can utter them. I want to hike in shady woods, along fishy blue streams. I know nothing of stone, ice, and this incessant wind, which plucks and tears at my jacket. Harsh breaths, endless. I begin to hate Steve and his one measured step after another. He climbs against an utterly blue heaven, upwards and upwards. This lasts, with two short rests, for six hours.

"There it is!" he shouts.

A few hundred feet above us, I see a tiny yellow box perched improbably in the very midst of the barren scree bowl. I nearly cry. I want to hug Steve ahead of me, Bill behind me, and I am embarrassed for feeling this way.

We decide not to go on, but to cache our food under some boulders right here. I sit down a moment, for the world has begun to spin. Surely, it's the world that's tipsy and not me. I try to make the horizon line of peaks come straight. Suddenly I feel sick and say, "I've got to get out of here."

Just at that moment, the four Peruvian porters who are working for the Italians appear above us, returning from their carry to Camp Berlin at 20,000 feet. Living in the high Cordillera Blanca, the brothers Los Angeles are already well acclimatized and joke with us as they pass by. I don't wait for my amigos. I join the Peruvians and copy what they do – shuffling my feet, I ski through the scree. A thousand feet, fifteen hundred feet, the pounding of my head hurries me along. We slip through the *nieves penitentes* and are back in camp. Pepi, the leader of the Italians, hands me a cup of tea, while one of his countrymen takes off my pack. I crawl into my sleeping bag and am instantly unconscious.

Near dusk I'm awakened by Steve and Bill. I peek out of my bag. The orange tent casts ghoulish light on our sweaty, dusty boots, on flashlights, food containers, open stuff sacks. Bill is sleeping. Steve is eating crackers. Noxzema is smeared on his cheeks, which are burnt red and raw except for the circles left by his sunglasses.

"How do you feel?" he says

I'm shocked to hear myself say, "Terrific."

The next day we lounge on the steps of the *refugio*, drinking one endless cup of tea and soup. The Austrians return from the summit, three big strong Aryans and a blond woman with thighs big as my waist. Bill looks at her and says, "She'd crack your head like a nut." They pack quickly and, without stopping to rest, descend. A dozen Americans roll in about an hour later. They are badly windburned, their lips sprout feversores, their packframes are piled haphazardly with gear; they look routed. Only half of them topped out during the windy previous day, and one of their unsuccessful members, Vera Watson, has remained at 20,000 feet to give it another try. We watch them disappear over the lip of the plateau, then gaze up the brown, imperturbable face of the mountain.

"They didn't take enough time to acclimatize," Steve says.

We try not to make a similar mistake. Eating, drinking, dozing in the refuge, we spin out the day. Late in the afternoon, Bill and I walk to the edge of the precipice, sit on a flat rock, and stare at the glaciers below. They climb towards the turrets rimming the edge of the cirque, over which clouds seem to pour like surf.

Bill, who drove a taxi in Denver for six months to take this trip, says, "My Dad's got this *National Geographic* atlas, and in his last letter he said he'd found Aconcagua and finally knew where I was."

"What's his name?"

"William, like me."

"And your Mom?"

"She's dead."

We cradle mugs of tea in our hands, our feet outstretched, the big climbing boots clumsy at the end of our legs. "About a year ago," says Bill, "I wrote my Dad this letter and told him not to expect much from me now, and we haven't had an argument since." He looks up at the sky filled with clouds. "Wish I'd told my mother that."

Plaza Mulas is the last haven. In the morning we repeat the climb to 17,000 feet, and, at the food cache, Steve stops for lunch. Bill and I continue up to the hut where Liske eats some cookies and immediately gets sick. He doesn't have the stomach or the energy to go back down to the cache, so I return alone and ferry up his load and mine. It destroys me. But there's no time to rest.

Steve and I chop a precarious platform for the tent, while Bill melts water in the hut. We stake down the tent with rocks the size of truck tires and finally have a moment to look around.

The scree bowl stretches from Plaza Mulas at 14,000 feet to just below the summit step at 22,000 feet – a gray bowl of stone and snow in the side of Aconcagua. In the center of it, on this tiny level spot, is a six-foot by six-foot box, fastened down with one-inch cable. Our tent is guyed with alpine cord.

Now that our work is done and I can see where we are, I stretch my back by raising my hands toward the sky. My fingers sink into the deep blueness, and the feeling of space and airiness becomes so intense that, for a second, I believe I can step off the tent platform and walk upon the summits of the peaks thousands of feet below. My mind is clean.

The moment doesn't last long. Aconcagua vanishes in the reddish dusk and it begins to snow. Then I see a figure stumble toward us.

"Vera Watson!" cries Steve, as she falls into our arms.

We push the American solo climber into the hut and zip her into her sleeping bag. While Bill tries to feed her tea and chocolate, she carries on about seeing ghosts on the summit.

The hut's too small for all of us; as soon as Vera comes around, Steve and I return to the tent and get a brew going for ourselves. The stove warms us. We share some chocolate, split an orange, eat cheese and crackers, then make some pea soup to wash down the tea. Despite the flapping of the tent walls, the world seems safe, comfortable, and lustrous, as if I were in a Christmas bulb and seeing Steve through the glow of a fireplace. We fall asleep.

Soon the tent begins to rise. Thinking that I'm having another oxygen-starved dream, I mumble, "Go back to sleep, lad." But the floor continues to come up between Steve and me; the center pole bends over at a frightening angle and nylon smothers me. NO DREAM! The walls of the tent sound like machine guns blasting. We're being blown off the mountain! A terrific gust flattens the tent and I roll toward Steve, who lunges, grabs the center pole and shouts, "Hold on! It's gonna go!"

It doesn't.

Vera goes down. We carry food to Camp Berlin at 20,000 feet, return to 17, sleep another windy night, then climb to 20,000, and occupy one of two tiny A-frame huts. There's just enough head room to sit up in our sleeping bags. We have an early dinner and, since I'm the last one to turn in, I fetch ice blocks for tomorrow morning's breakfast. After arranging the pot and stove by the door, I get in my bag, only to discover I'm too excited to fall asleep. Will we go to the summit tomorrow?

I look at my two friends, already asleep, without whom I wouldn't be here. Zinc oxide covers their beards and the remains of dinner lie in their moustaches. Their bleached hair strays from their hats, and their noses are burnt a brownish-purple by the wind. Every few minutes one of them stops breathing for several seconds, then takes a deep, rattling gasp, which compensates for the missed breath. It's called Cheyne-Stokes breathing and affects everyone at altitude.

I put on my gloves, pull my balaclava over my ears, snuggle deeper into my bag and, lying on my back, look out the tiny window of the refugio. The sun is sinking over the Andes and into the line of deeper blue which indicates the Pacific Ocean, one hundred miles away. I feel as if I'm an astronaut, floating outside the airy skin of the planet. The sun sets; the horizon grows wounded red; the mountains bloom gentian clouds. Snow blows across the window and a whistle hangs in the gable. As the first star appears, I feel the curve of the planet bend my spine.

I look below, to the glacial rivers, meandering toward the plains. Like my writing, they have become a hieroglyphic. They lead me to a green place. They pull at my heartstrings. They tell me a secret I cannot yet decipher.

No summit attempt. Strong winds. We hang tight all day in the hut, battered. The Italians went for the top, got turned back by temperatures far below zero. We watch them descend, limping with frostbite.

Steve and I manage some tea, soup and crackers at lunch, but Bill doesn't stir from his sleeping bag. In fact, he doesn't even take off his glacier glasses. In his balaclava he looks like a dead Arthurian knight. When we ask if he's alright, he says to just bury him here.

After dinner (mostly liquid), Steve and I go outside to watch the sun set. The needle of the anemometer on the hut has run off the scale at 100 kilometers per hour. We huddle behind a rock. The sun sets, and sets, and sets while flaming orange cloud-waves, torn by the wind, leap up through the Cordillera. I punch Steve in the shoulder. A moment to remember: the two of us at 20,000 feet in the Andes.

He grins. He's gotten the same flash: we're actually climbing the biggest mountain in the hemisphere. He goes to the hut and yells: "Bill, come out and see the sunset."

No reply.

"Liske," he yells again. "Come out here. You'll never see another sunset like this in your life."

No reply.

"Liske! You'll probably never be up this high again." From the hut, a faint croak: "Bet your ass."

We rise at four. At last the wind has died. We melt ice for tea, eat some oatmeal, and put on our boots last, having kept them in our sleeping bags to prevent them from freezing solid. It is sixteen below zero. As we crawl from the hut, Liske says, "Hang on a second." He goes back in and keeps Andrews and me stomping in the cold for twenty minutes while he readjusts his supergaiters. "Goddamn Liske," I mutter. My toes are freezing.

By a silver of moon and the haze from the stars, we climb up a buttress. My secondhand boots are a bit too small and I've put on one pair too many socks. My toes grow numb. But there's no place to stop. On we go – up, up the ridge, cresting its top just as the sun rises from the pampa and the peaks below us turn a warm yellow. Then we see it to the west: flung over the Cordillera, hanging in the sky and reaching out across the ocean, is a gigantic pyramid-shadow. Indigo, top trailing a snowplume, it's Aconcagua!

When we reach a level spot, I have to stop and warm my feet. I remove my boots and take my toes in my hands. Steve gently takes my feet and puts them on his bare stomach. Then Bill does the same.

"How you doing?" I say to Liske.

"Fine," he says, wincing from the cold.

When I can feel my toes, we take a minute to share a frozen orange and drink some water. Even this tiny bit of food sits in our throats. No one suggests we don't go on. We climb a snowridge and start across the top of the Gran Acarreo, which funnels to the summit through a couloir called the Canaleta Final. Below us we spy a huddled form. It's the dead Japanese climber, but we're too far away to see his smile.

On we go. Hood up, eyes at my feet, I forget Steve ahead of me and Bill behind. There seems to be no air left on the earth and that which I do manage to breathe has no life-giving O_2. We begin to cross an interminable scree slope. I know this is wrong, that we should have gone up along the left rock wall. I know this from the talk I have heard at the mountaineering club in Mendoza, where we looked at pictures of the route, and because it feels intuitively right. But Steve is the leader and always correct. I'm tired, Bill's tired, we stumble in the scree. After an hour of creeping along at 22,000 feet, we stop and have a conference. Steve goes ahead and reconnoiters a narrow gully. He yells to us that it rises to the summit. I yell to him that I think it's the other way. Steve comes back, disappointed, exhausted, sits down. Bill reconnoiters the other way while I sit, exhausted. He yells that his gully is cleaner and will go, and he begins to climb the left-hand rocks. Steve and I go up the right side of Bill's gully and traverse a snowslope. Steve kicks steps. I follow and balance with my ax. The slope becomes steep; Steve uses his ski pole for support. I must be looking spacey for he asks me if I remember how to use an ax. I repeat the techniques of self-arrest. Things seem to be getting foolish. We climb; the couloir steepens; it's a long way down to the bottom, which is studded with rocks. I look out: the peaks fall away to the horizon and the sky is curved, as if I'm viewing the world through a wide angle lens. I continue to kick

steps. The snow squeaks in places. We get to a rock ledge, pause.
Steve turns around; his face, caked with zinc-oxide, looks like a
clown's. "We should have been roped," he says. I smile. I'm beginning to lose his voice. We climb. On the other side of the couloir I
see Bill climbing, sitting, watching us with a drawn expression,
his mouth hanging slack. I try to keep Steve's pace, but can't. I try
to regulate my breathing – a breath a step. But I fail. I begin to
take three breaths a step, then five. I remember what one of the
Italians said when he returned from his summit attempt: "I was
talking to the rocks." I remember what Vera said: "I crawled."
Then I remember nothing. Sometimes I see Steve's blue overmitt
gesturing toward the summit. But looking up disorients me, as
the pounding of my heart pulses glittering black drops across the
heaven. Most of the time I see only the rocks in which I stumble;
there's a fog between my temples. Steve reaches down, gives me
a hand over a difficult place, and tells me that I can wait here and
he and Bill will come down for me. I tell him that I can't stop
now – when I'm this close. My voice sounds weak, far away. I
clench my fist and say, "Think, concentrate." And I'm lying on my
back again. But I slowly right myself, crawl a ways, stand up,
climb on, deciding that I shall get to the top of this mountain or
die. Steve's boots are above me, always out of reach; I never catch
up. I lean on my ax. How much longer can this last? I make a few
moves, bump into Steve's leg, stop, wait. He nudges me. He's
going to tell me to pace myself. He nudges me again. I pull back
my hood and see him pointing. The summit is ten steps away,
and Bill – ski pole extended over his head in triumph – is twirling,
twirling against the lowering clouds. "Come on," says Steve, and
he links arms with me, just as he did on our training hike in
Bolivia when, only a few hundred yards from the road, we
stepped onto a snowy hill and he said, "Until Aconcagua, Señor."
We take the last half-a-dozen feet slowly, almost reluctantly, then
rush to meet Bill who falls into our arms – our three heads together, fists pounding each other's backs. I'm weeping but there
aren't any tears. There's nothing to see but rocks, a cross and the
clouds. It begins to snow. We try to take some pictures, then
Steve helps me into my parka and mittens. He says, "It's six-
thirty." Have we been going for fourteen hours? "Let's get out of
Dodge," he orders. We drop off the summit and start down

through boulders and snow. Is this the way we came? It can't be. My legs become loose and uncontrollable between the rocks; far-away voices call to me as I slip, fall, and slide, the words "eonia" and "familia" falling and sliding through my oxygen-starved brain. It snows harder. We can't see where we're going. Bill leads through the gloom. Steve steps on a rock that gives way; he trips and falls, recovers before sliding; limps. I fall, catch myself. He lets me lean on him. I stumble again. Steve calls a halt, says in a stern, frightened voice, "Are you rational?" Before I can answer, Bill says, "Listen, I want to get out of here." Steve lectures: "Listen, we have at the most four hours of daylight to get back to the hut. You stay out here tonight and you'll die. Now, are you going to try?" "I am trying," I say. But my voice shocks me. It comes from eons away. I've never been lectured to before. How did this happen to me? "Okay," I say deliberately. "I'll . . . be . . . careful." Three steps down, I trip and go flying headfirst down the slope. But my buddies are ahead of me and the only one to hold onto is a rock. I grab it as I slide by, flip around, steady myself, then follow after their two dim shapes. Somehow, we reach the bottom of the Canaleta. Liske crouches and hangs his head between his knees. "I'm not exhausted," he says. "That happened hours ago." He pushes on the snow, struggles upright, and stumbles down the ridge. Steve gets behind me and, cajoling, joking, ex-horting, keeps me on Bill's tail. Faster we go, the dusk pushing us. We reach the level spot where we warmed my feet and can see the drop-off of the ridge, below which is the hut. I go over to a snowdrift, undo my windpants, and become oblivious to night coming on. The snowdrift changes from dull white to pink to gray before my eyes and still I don't rise from my crouch. Liske yells, "Did you die?" I come back. He sees my fouled hand, which I'm cleaning with snow and says, "You get the Aconcagua brown-palm award." And for the first time since . . . yesterday . . . we grin.

The air seems thick, heavy, fills my lungs. Carefully, we work our way down the buttress. It's dark, ten-thirty, when we reach the hut. We melt some ice on the stove. Steve has cocoa; I have tea. Bill is already snoring. Then I am *in the sky. Over the North Atlantic. Flying alone. My arms are spread and I can see the dark shape of Newfoundland below, without a single light, all dark and pregnant. I reach into my pockets and fling golden stars onto the empty land. Cities light where there were forests, and I walk toward their glow, along loops of highway. It's early morning and I walk toward my grandfather's white house, the oak tree, the croquet lawn. My brother and sister are sitting on the grass among the mallets and balls, and I wade to them through waist-deep snow. P.V. hugs me and my sister touches my arms. I want to tell them about the stars, but I kiss her and walk on toward school and a writing class. A wonderful idea looms just as the bell rings, ending our writing period. I sneak away because I can't hand in these notes.*

I go home, work on the assignment. But it's Sunday evening in the old white house. I sit on the sofa and write on the coffee table, while across the room my grandfather sits in his rocker and reads the paper. The front door opens and my Mom and Dad come in, followed by the smell of the Sunday city—cold perfume, smoke, and something sad. They say, "To bed! It's Monday tomorrow. School."

I wake in the dawn and work on my essay, but it's not ready by the time I leave the house. I can't hand it in. I walk toward a coffee shop and sit on a stool and wait for Dad, who comes in wearing his black overcoat and the Tyrolean hat I brought him years ago. He has a newspaper folded under his arm, folded in half top to bottom, as he has carried it every day of his working life. He sits next to me and says, "What are you doing here?" His coattails hang off the back of the stool.

I want to tell him about the stars, but say nothing.

He stands up and walks away. I follow. He walks along a wide avenue, under the morning shadows of the buildings, under some trees where he stops and says, "I'd like to see the stars alone." He looks at me and I obey him.

I walk away, away . . . a long, long time away . . . until I'm walking back into the city, the loops of highway behind my shoulders. It's very early morning, the sky pale, and I walk down Main Street from high up where it's a dirt road. I walk down into town and see buildings standing above me and one last park below, all empty and quiet in the morning. I sit down on a bench, under a maple tree and wait for my father. But the morning brightens and he never arrives.

It's a smoky blue dawn, covered with snow. We descend the

switchbacks below Plaza Mulas, retrace our way through the boulder fields, the moraine, ford the river, hike the steep valley trail, and arrive at our first camp at dusk. Green grass, the lake, a mild breeze – we drop our packs and look back to the summit of Aconcagua in the clouds.

Sign
Of The Fishes

Junin de los Andes, as dusty a town as you'd care to see, lies at
the base of the cordillera in the Lake District of Argentina.
All of its dirt streets eventually meet on a square filled with
pine trees and a large gazebo. Land Rovers cough on the streets,
kicking up the stones while from the open doors of restaurants
the sound of fast guitars and the voices of singing gauchos leap,
punctuating the cool autumn air.

Along the edge of town the Rio Chimehuin flows. Willow bor-
ders it, cow pastures too, and in these quiet meadows tall chest-
nut horses gaze sagaciously over the kine. The Hosteria Chimehuin also edges to the banks of the river and sometimes, when
the sun was high at the midday, I'd walk through the courtyard
and into the snug dining room. A fire would be turning to white
ash in the hearth and the girl servant, her straw-colored hair
pulled back like the wickers of a cottage broom, would be done
with most of her lunchtime chores.

She often made me a double espresso and put a cake on the
table with it. She said the cake was a *regalito*, a little gift, and

charged me the cost of our conversation for the coffee, though out of habit she stood while we talked. We discussed Mendoza, where she had been born and I had climbed a big mountain, and Junin, where she had come to start a new life and I had come, of course, to hike and fish for trout.

Behind our table hung photographs of the renowned fishermen who had stayed at the Hosteria. Among the fishermen pictured were Charlie Ritz and Joe Brooks and Al McClane. Their smiles were as large as the ten-kilo trout they held.

The straw-haired girl poured me another cup of coffee, that particular afternoon, and wished me luck for the evening's fishing. She used to worry about my sleeping under the sky and wading the river in only shorts, worried that I might catch cold. She told me, "Someday I hope you are rich. Then you will return and take a room at the Hosteria."

In the late afternoon I worked up the river, the valley wide and filled with sun. I cast as I went, concentrating on my style: stiff wrist, stop the rod at one o'clock, wait until the line unrolls, drive forward smoothly. Fly fishing is the most difficult angling technique to master, requiring strict attention to details. When done correctly – the angler exerting just the right amount of force – even the longest cast appears to have been accomplished without any great expenditure of energy.

Soon I began to see enticing pools upriver and instead of stalking them properly I tried to double haul, an advance cast used to throw the line long distances. My line began to collapse in a tangle; I snapped off a fly and, on the next cast, hooked myself in the back of the ear. This was nothing new. When I had begun to fly fish I had expected immediate proficiency, was quickly disappointed and, like many of us when faced with something difficult, chose an easier course: I was lured away by spinning and baitcasting, each of which promised long casts and more fish in the short run.

Despite my lack of discipline, I had never completely given up fly fishing. It was too intriguing, too graceful a sport to ever abandon, and, I must admit, any time I used a fly rod, it transformed the most ordinary stream into a wild river.

I continued up the Chimehuin, which narrowed and quickened as it rose into the front range of the Andes. I spotted some promising water and kept my casts short and neat. The streamer flashed through the green chutes and as my line straightened they hit. One was better than three pounds. Then, just as the sun was a half-circle above the mountains, the rod jerked in my hands. A large silver fish leapt from the stream, hit the water, and fled. I ran after him, along the rocky bank, the tiny reel protesting. Upside down, suspended against the sun, the trout leapt again, and my fly came back to me, lazily through the twilight.

I walked to the road and started hiking toward Junin. At the crossroads a hitchhiker was standing. We greeted each other. He was French, almost fifty years old by the wrinkles around his eyes, much younger in his smile, and was dressed in corduroy slacks and a neat white shirt. A small knapsack leaned against his leg. We exchanged pleasantries awhile, then retired to the cafe for a beer.

For seventeen years the French hitchhiker had been a math teacher in North Africa. He had recently come to South America and was presently living in Buenos Aires. However, he made it clear that he no longer worked at teaching.

"What work do you do?" I asked, being polite.

He held out his hitchhiker's thumb. "My work." He had been to Tierra del Fuego and back and planned to go to Venezuela. He worked mostly all the time now, he said, and asked me, moving his head in the direction of my rod, if my work went well. "The work goes very well," I said, and I described the trout I had released and the one I had lost. We clinked glasses.

In the morning I sat by the Rio Chimehuin, ate my breakfast, and tied some new leaders. The sun was warm upon and sparkled on the rapids. Behind me the pastures awoke with hazy yawns. I ate an apple, sliced and dipped in wheat germ, and some gouda, still cold from the night. Then I drank a cup of black coffee cooked on my small gas stove. This was my standard breakfast, and I always enjoyed it – the freshness of the apple contrasted against the milkiness of the cheese, the astrigency of the coffee washing it all down.

When finished, I slung my pack on and started out of town toward the crossroads. I was planning to hitch to the Rio Malleo and then walk along it, to its confluence with the Rio Aluminé. I had read in the Hosteria's copy of *McClane's Fishing Encyclopedia* that at this confluence, far from any road, was a large pool where possibly the largest brown trout of Argentina lived.

The air was cool, my pack pleasant; the mountains were feathered with their first snow. Behind the foothills the Voclan Lanin rose, a white 13,000-foot tetrahedron against the blue sky, which a week before I had climbed with two fine friends who had now returned to the States. The morning dawned in my lungs. It was a good day to be alive.

By midday it wasn't. It was cold; it was windy; only three cars had passed. I had my usual two o'clock falling out with South America.

It was apparent, however, that more traffic was going in the opposite direction. I dug out my road map and saw that the Chimehuin, which I was standing near, also met the Aluminé, south of the Malleo. Surely there would be a great confluence and large trout there. I could also see that the road I was on would leave me about a day's walk from this confluence. Cursing McClane for having biased me, wishing I had something besides a Texaco road map for my hike, feeling indecisive, I walked to the other side of the road.

After a few hours an old Falcon compact came along. As it went by, the two men inside gestured to their overloaded back seat. I threw them a pleading wave; they slowed and returned.

I saw fishing rod cases in the rear window and, when the passenger opened the door, two elderly men. Both had stiff, short moustaches, the kind worn by British diplomats and field marshals during the Thirties. We began to speak Spanish, but soon fell into English.

"You looked so terribly disappointed," the driver said as I made room for myself on the rear seat, "we had to stop." He wore a sea-blue sweater and smoked a high-bowled, stodgy pipe. His eyes were like the diamonds in a curling wave and his hair was a tangle of clouds. Beneath his sweater he was thickset, shaped like his pipe. He looked like a sea captain.

The other man was slightly built, and though he had obviously been fishing most of the day, his khaki shirt was impeccably clean. Below his curving Arabic nose and soft yellow eyes, he sported a slim blond version of the driver's white moustache.

The dashboard was covered with maps, tobacco pouches, loose cigarettes, and a shapeless woolen cap. Big trout flies – muddler minnows, maribous – were hooked into its brim. Mackinaws were piled on the seat and on top of them was a picnic basket stuffed with gloves, a thermos, a pint of whiskey, and the remains of a large chicken.

The driver must have caught my glance, for he told me to take some whiskey. After we had had a round of snorts, we began to talk about the fishing, but hardly had I said a sentence and the slim man replied with the beginnings of a nod, when the driver interrupted with, "Caught an eight pound brown this morning. By a friend's house, private grounds, lovely fish. On a black fly. Lovely fish. He – augh, augh, acha, uhaa! . . . Never smoke, my lad, never." He rolled down his window and spat. His friend, after the driver had regained his composure and returned his concentration to the road, added, "Yes. A lovely fish."

Their English was so faultless that I remarked on it. The driver explained, "When I was in the Argentine Embassy in London, I met a girl to whom I became engaged, and later married, by the way. She would invite me to dinner, and her father spoke horrible Spanish, so they would always talk English around the dinner table. My English was as wretched as her father's Spanish, so I bought myself Fowler's grammar book. I think it was my discipline that won her heart. You know the English."

I mentioned that I did, having gone to university in London. He asked in what had I read. I answered literature and philosophy. Like a knee jerk the two men replied, "Better than engineering."

Then the driver asked, "What work do you do now?"

I said, "I fish."

He asked if I had ever heard of Joe Brooks. I replied yes, and he recounted how he and Brooks and Curt Gowdy had made a ninety-minute program at Lake General Paz. "For the ABC television network. We were trying to break the world record for brook trout, but, alas, we failed. I think the days of the glorious fish are gone."

His tone of dismay moved me to ask how the fishing compared to that of, say, thirty years ago, and he said, "You're too late, my boy. The Spooner Rooners have killed it. Blast the bastards! With their treble hooks everywhere."

"Why do you say that?"

"I've lived on Lago Traful for years, and they've killed it, those grapplers."

"But people tell me it still has good trolling."

He began to scratch his chest, saying, "I get itchy when I hear the word. Trolling!" He twitched his shoulders convulsively. "Can't stand it. Only time I do it is when the wife asks for a fish for dinner, and then I troll with a fly. I did an experiment once with a grandson. He used a streamer fly, I a spoon of *nácar*; how you say?"

"Mother of pearl," I supplied.

"Yes, mother of pearl. And he outfished me ten to one."

While we had been talking, the driver had begun to rub his knee. Suddenly he cried, "Damn rheumatism! Holding down the accelerator aggravates it. Used to wade streams like you, in shorts, and am now paying for it. You'll pay for it too, but you don't think of that now. One never does. This is the highest mesa around," he interrupted himself as we reached the top of our climb. "A magnificent view of the country."

We gazed across the *llanura*, the yellow plains of Argentina, to the Andes and the purple western sky. The car rolled into the valley of the Chimehuin; the mountains were lost to sight, and we began to talk of the country: of the Argentine, its political troubles, and its mixture of many peoples. I remarked that it was unfortunate that the gaucho had disappeared, taking with him the romance of the pampa.

"Oho, but you're wrong." The driver shook his head. "He's still here and as proud and honest as ever. And thank God we have him! When he goes, the shambles will be complete. One thing you should know, for it might be useful, and it will tell you something of his character. You should never hail a gaucho, for is that any way to call a man, as if yelling at a dog? You must walk up to him, and talk to him, and he will respect you for it. And if approaching his house, never gallop up, but walk your horse the last two hundred meters. Do you know why? . . . I didn't think so. To allow his women to dress their hair, which is only civilized, you know. They have some fine customs."

We watched the river wind by our left side. It wound under red cliffs, under banks dense with pine, the river aquamarine through poplars turning gold with autumn. The driver remarked on this – the color of the poplars – and how it was sad that the fishing in the Chimehuin was "washed up" and I had missed it. His friend disagreed, saying that, after all, I was hiking to a rarely fished section of the river. But the driver didn't answer, and they left it at that.

As we drove along, I began to hope that the driver would invite me to his house on Lago Traful. I wanted to fish with him, to talk into the night. I wanted a roof over my head and a bed to sleep in.

But at the crossroads we parted – they south to Traful, I to walk the Chimehuin. We exchanged names. The driver's was Tito and his friend's Poncho. Tito said it was too bad I couldn't come along to the next junction, for he knew of an excellent cafe there, and we could have had a double espresso and a ham and cheese sandwich, which they made very well.

"But of course," he added, as he slowed to let me out, "you must go on. It's your time to be keen."

Dusk found me along the river, and I missed the only strike I had. The night fell and the mesas were transformed into dark rectangles beneath the stars. I spread my tarp against the wind, ate some pea soup, a small can of sardines, and drank a cup of tea. The river talked of the mountains it had recently lived in, and the wind of snow and far spaces.

I awoke; the morning was tungsten blue, and it happened, by coincidence or portent, to be my birthday – Pisces, the sign of the fishes. I wondered how to recognize it. Finally I said, "Good fishing, Señor." I tied on a yellow bucktail, put on damp shorts, and entered the pool below camp. The water was numbing.

The wind being still, I made a few lovely casts, the long S of green line tight and singing. As the freezing water pulled at my thighs and sprayed my arms, I thought of the people close to me – the people who would think of me on my birthday and probably wouldn't understand how happy I was. My rod tightened at the strike, and my leader parted.

I ate breakfast, broke camp, and made off downstream. The sun grew hot and through the sandy pampa clumped with grass, I walked ten or twelve kilometers. I passed several small herds of cattle, a few flocks of sheep, and a gaggle of brant that rose like a white blanket before me. Jack rabbits sprang from beneath my feet and jigged laconically away. Mostly I passed crumbling bones and parched rock, a few bloody bird feathers and the lizards sunning. The sound of the river to my left was reassuring. I knew that as long as I continued downstream I'd eventually reach the Aluminé.

When the sun crossed my meridian, I angled back to the water, took off my boots, hung my feet in a pool, and had some lunch – a bit of salami, a piece of Brie-like cheese, a slice of onion. I had dessert as well: some biscuits and a square of chocolate. The chocolate was the only sweet I carried, and, because it was the only one, a dessert of it was sweet indeed.

I continued to hike, the pack, after all those months-upon-mountain-months, simply there and heavy. Although I was enjoying the starkly yellow, spare-green land, I became lonely – for the friends I had climbed with, for someone like Tito to fish with, for my solitary way across the arid mesa country. My walk to the confluence became purposeless.

I felt the pang, its rending was a reward, and I thought, it's been a long solitary time southward, this fifteen-month cleansing, this experiment in using time differently. I'm happy with it and when I've gone far enough to satisfy my curiosity, I'll return and see the people who often live in my thoughts: Booth, my university friend, with whom I've hunted many woods; my brother P.V., with whom I grew among the fish of the north and who's my companion on the sea – the two men who've never forgotten the times we spent together – and of course the rest of the family, who by separation have become dear.

And then I thought, perhaps it's all about this: each of us is given some seventy years, a decent amount of time and such a niggardly small gift when you have the eyes to see the gifts you must leave. In that time you shouldn't be afraid to take out a year or two or even more to do something not in the straight path you originally chose. You shouldn't be afraid to watch the slow turning of stars and clouds and strange peoples, for although family, country, and abiding loves will never afterwards be holy, they will have become tender and subtle in unimagined ways.

Understanding this for the first time, not in my head but as miles beneath my feet, I knew what could not be avoided: to work and to sweat, to be in pain of body, mind, and heart, especially the pain, for it would be the only way a goal became sweet. "So walk hard my friend," I told myself, "walk hard and grin in small laughter when it hurts even to cry, when you crave to lie and sleep, for there'll be nothing but the long sleep afterwards."

During the remainder of the afternoon, I hiked over desolate mesas without catching sight of the river. Behind me were the Andes – gray, stern, snowcapped – around me nothing but yellow burnt hills, sage grass, the skeleton of a sheep. I ran out of water; a lone hawk circled in the sky; I felt unkindred and alone.

I climbed a mesa that looked like every other mesa I had climbed, and I came in view of the river again. Willows lined the banks; glittering water interlaced the sandbars; a row of poplars marched up a hillside. In the heat waves the distant mountains shimmered. A slight breeze moved the grass; the flies buzzed – life was close. My head began to pound: death seemed close as well, and precious, and as unimportant as my old age.

Across the valley, downstream from where I stood, another large river joined the Chimehuin. I was sure it was the Aluminé and that this was the *confluencia* to which I had been hiking.

I reached the other side of the river by fording – up to my waist in the rapids – and I was glad that I had had the foresight to cut a wading staff. I would have been swept away if I hadn't.

I made camp, drank the sweet water, bathed and lay naked in the sun. Then I walked over a delta of round stones to the rivers' joining. I waded into the water and with a fly tied in New Hampshire cast into the eddies. Suddenly a rainbow vaulted into the air as if to take a look at the upper world, but he was at the end of my line.

I caught another and lost some, then hooked a large fish that fought powerfully. I brought the brown trout to shore, looked once at his orange flanks, and decided to return him. The sun was briefly down, the mesas were carmine, and I was pleased.

By the light of the fire I sat. It was a wonderful fire, made of dead willow that burned a long time. The river rushed deep and strong behind the flames and there wasn't another light in the valley of the Chimehuin. The stars shone brightly in the heaven and I could see the Milky Way and the Pleiades.

I ate a can of meat fried in butter and the rest of my chocolate bar, then some biscuits. The chocolate was bittersweet and cut the tongue; the biscuits were a wafer of vanilla taste, seemingly bland, blandly memorable. Together they were outstanding. I had planned on saving them for the following day, but it was my birthday and birthdays do not come every year.

I gazed at Crux, which is the cross of the southern sky, and after a while took out my pad and began to write of the trout and of my stay in the Lake District. It soon was time to tie new leaders and to see what flies I had left. It had been time to do that time ago, but of all things I love I love this the most, the casting of words in the rivers of my days.

As I slipped into my sleeping bag, the night's cool air was rare and I felt graceful. I was alone and silent along the sound of the water, at ease in the creation, having come a long way to this confluence, my rivers wide and tender for their journey's rigor.

Beggar

There are beggars out in Quito and I don't know what to do about them.

They plague me. They are fibroids in my lungs and I am choking.

They haunt me. From the end of a coal-black tunnel their eyes gleam at me like the nuggets of a motherlode.

What can I do for them?

What *should* I do for them?

I think I know. But I prefer not to answer.

When I first walked through Quito on my way back North, I observed them. Then my heart grew soft and I gave them alms. Last week I reverted to an old ploy of mine: I began to photograph them, as if preserving them on Kodachrome would honor their lives of rags and garbage.

Yes, they fascinate me.

How, I ask myself, does a human being become reduced to a heap of tatters and cancers?

Look at them: First the thin man who sits upon the steps of the cathedral. His face is split by a line of shadow and sunlight, and his hair is prematurely gray, the same stone gray as his jacket, which is two sizes too large. His hands rest on his knees—one of which is missing, as is the leg below it. He spends a few minutes looking toward the street and the passersby, then turns his face to the interior of the church.

I stare at him too long and when he looks back to the sidewalk he sees my eyes: concerned, curious, troubled. I depress the shutter and his face vanishes as the mirror of my camera snaps up. I turn away.

But there are beggars everywhere: the white-haired char-woman, drooling and muttering curses at the entrance to the train station; the blind man wearing a civil defense helmet; the boy with the clubfoot; the leper.

Stop. I can't bear to describe another. I won't take another picture. I refuse to be a photojournalist any longer.

But then what can I do?

I think I know. But I prefer not to answer.

I've been down here too long to be objective about my own health. Down in the mines of South America among the junk of the Incas, the Conquistadores, and my dissolute English and Irish cousins. Fifteen months I've been filling my prospector's sack with precious nuggets—great fish, tall mountains, eternal friends—and haven't noticed the creeping silicosis.

Oh, I've taken the standard palliatives: I've given my copper coins to the little Mexican girls in the Zocalo; to the urchins of Valparaiso; to the shoeshine boy who jumped into the sunlight of Panama's Avenida Balboa and shouted, "Mister! Hey mister, gimme a dime."

But the morphine shot of my charity couldn't stop the pain when Quito's one-legged man called out, "*Un otro sucre por favor.*"

Why the hell did he ask for more?

I was almost on the jet. I was ready to leave my Yukon with the riches I had. I could have left this continent shaped like a cornucopia or a seraphim's trumpet without a backward glance.

If he hadn't called out for more. What more could I have given him?

I think I know. But I prefer not to answer.

Damn it! I was almost in the daylight and safe when he called out. I looked back only once. But I knew I saw it – another motherlode.

It's not easy to dress as a beggar. Even the cheapest market clothing looks appealing compared to the rags on a beggar's back.

I took my new cotton trousers, my blue poncho, and sandals to the dump and dirtied them. Then I cut them a little with my pocket knife. I bought some crutches, hung my small camera around my neck, and left my hotel with my costume in a paper bag. In a washroom stall of the train station, I changed, rubbing some of the dirt I'd brought along in an envelope on my face and hair. I also stained my nails with some grease. Then I wrapped a rag and air splint around my foot and hobbled from the stall. As I left the washroom, I glanced into the mirror. The transformation was complete. I was abject. My first reaction wasn't repulsion. It was fear. But I walked into the sunshine and limped down the street. Not a person looked at me.

At the cathedral I stood at the foot of the steps. The sunshine had left the side of the church; the man in the herringbone coat had turned his collar up and was dozing. I held out my fedora, upside down, and within an hour I had collected three sucres.

Then the man with one leg said, "This is my spot."

I acted as if I hadn't heard him.

"You can't have been here very long," he added. "Everyone has a spot that no one else can take. Go to the front, which is for everyone."

"I've been there," I said. "There are too many others, and besides, I'm down here and you're up there."

He leaned forward and peered at me sharply. "Where are your from?" he said.

"Tulcan."

"Then go back there."

I hung my head and looked at the ground. He continued to stare at me. "I won't take your spot," I said. "But I'm tired of standing. Could I sit a minute?"

He said nothing, and so I climbed the steps and settled myself by his side, about three feet between us. "It would have been better," I said, "if I'd never come to Quito and worked on the highway."

"I saw the posters," he said.

"I worked only three days. A culvert got away and hit me."

I felt the camera resting against my chest and watched his face—the lean cheeks and long thin nose against the gray backdrop of the stone balustrade.

"You had an accident as well," I began.

"Being born," he said, his voice like a cleaver. "Don't try to make the time pass. I told you this is my spot."

I looked at my hands. "They say I might need an operation."

"Go back to Tulcan," he said.

"Nothing there."

"*Nada?*"

"*Nada.*"

He shook his head and gave a tiny shrug.

I picked up my crutch, laid it down. "How did you get here?" I said.

"I . . ." Taken off guard, he tilted his head to one side. "You mean how did this happen to me?"

"Yes," I said.

"It was circumstance," he said, and he didn't mean "luck" or "fate." "What can you do about that," he added, making a gesture with his hand as if sweeping away something done and not worth talking about. I thought I would hear no more, then, unexpectedly, he said, "I was a child when it happened. A cow kicked me in the leg and broke the bone. It healed but was never very strong. When my father died . . ." He stopped and looked at me suspiciously.

Knowing what he was thinking, that I was just leading him on, I said, "I won't stay. *Seguro.*"

He snorted; looked at his missing leg.

"*Seguro.*"

He watched the passersby. I let him be, and after a while I asked, "What happened when your father died?"

His chest rose, but he didn't sigh. He looked at his missing leg again, he looked at my crutches, and finally he looked at me. His eyes were a light yellow brown.

"I took over the land we had," he said. "A hillside. My sister had died with her second child, and my brother had gone down to the coast. My wife and I worked it ourselves. We had some pigs. Then my leg became weaker." He looked down at his hands, which were still farmer's hands. "It had to be cut off."

I looked at his leg and I noticed that he was looking at it as well. "She killed our pigs." he said, "one by one and sold them in the market. One Saturday night she didn't come back from town." He looked at me, raised his right hand, and pushed aside some air, implying that it was all over and done. "She came back," he said, "a few times." He nodded. "Then I came to Quito. I thought I could find work inside. Some little thing. But I could find nothing except the banana line. You don't know that, do you?"

I shook my head.

"The bananas come from Guayaquil on a freight train. They arrive twice a week, and anyone who needs money can work unloading them. I stood in line and took the bunches from the man on my left and passed them to the man on my right. Five hours a day, twice a week. Then my good leg couldn't hold me any longer."

I waited for more, but he only stared at the shadow climbing the building opposite us.

"You came here then?"

He turned his head slowly and looked at me. I felt stupid.

"I asked if I could sweep out the pews, clean the candle tray, any little thing. One father told me that nothing needed to be done, but I could sit outside with the others. As I walked outside another father, younger than the first, touched me on the shoulder and said, 'We have a man sweeping up. When he leaves you should ask again.' That was . . . months ago."

The sun had gone behind the cathedral, and the buildings across the way were shadowed. The man looked at my leg. "What a shame you ruined it," he said. "There's good money on the highway. Didn't you make anything?"

"I worked only a few days."

"A shame," he said.

I stared at my hands. I had about twenty-dollars worth of sucres under my poncho. I wanted to give them to him. In my hotel room I had a couple hundred dollars in cash. I wanted to give it to him as well. What would that solve?

I stood up and hobbled down the street. I almost went to my hotel. For the money? For my plane ticket and the safety of the jet? I don't know.

As I passed the market, I smelled broiling meat. I hadn't eaten since yesterday and stopped at a few stalls. I bought a leg of pork, two bottles of juice, a loaf of bread, and some oranges. I put it all in a paper sack, then limped back up the street to the one-legged man.

Of course, he was still there – gray hair, too large jacket, the empty pant leg, all alone on the steps of the cathedral.

I sat down next to him. He showed no surprise. I took the food out of the bag and said, "Here, let's eat."

"Where did you steal this?" he said.

"I had a few sucres left."

I took out my knife, handed it to him, and he began to cut strips of pork off the leg. I made a sandwich, then watched him take turns at the fruit, the bread, and the meat. He finished it all, saving his bottle of *naranjada* for last. He made a sucking noise as he emptied it and put it by his side on the step. He left his hand around it, as if holding something comfortable.

The street was empty and behind us the inner doors of the church swung shut. A few candles still burnt in the tray.

The man looked up at the sky, which was growing dark. I looked up at the sky with him. In a little while his head nodded toward his chest. I huddled deeper inside my poncho and dozed.

Shivering, I awoke, and didn't know where I was. I stared down the street to the roofs of the houses above which the mountains rose into the sky. Then the shivering of the man distracted me. He was bent over and held his hands on his stomach as he rocked back and forth. He touched his lips to the back of his hand.

I felt the camera against my chest, but it wasn't the picture to take home. I sat, watching him rock, and knew what I had to do.

I pulled the poncho over my head and wrapped it over his shoulders. He started under my arm and his eyes, instead of being silver-gray and gleaming, full of gratitude as I had expected, became like those of a deer when you've killed him: when you've stalked him far into the dusk, have shot well and the hunt is over; when you're standing above the dying animal – can actually see the light going down in his pupils – and, from deep within that wounded light, he asks your triumph, "Why?"

I dropped my arm and slid away from him. I don't know why I bothered with the crutches. But I got them under my arms and hobbled down the steps.

"Tulcanano," he called. Perhaps it was only to return my knife.

But I couldn't face him and that night caught the big bird to the States.

Traversing the Brooks Range of Alaska.

North

Who will prefer the jingle of jade pendants if
He once has heard stone growing in a cliff!

Laotzu

Excerpt from THE CHINESE TRANSLATIONS by Witter Bynner. Copyright © 1979 by
Witter Bynner. Reprinted by permission of Farrar, Straus and Giroux, Inc.

Hill Music

The last in line, as usual. Too many flowers to bend over, vistas to stare at . . . into . . . through. Too much tundra. Depending on his inclination, a person can try to cover lots of it each day, reaching for the horizon, or he can wander, head bent and eyes swiveling, grazing, so to speak, over the country.

North Slope, Arctic Circle, Brooks Range, Alaska: way up on the hemisphere, walking east toward the Yukon. The ocean sits left and the mountains right, both covered with ice. Hard to get lost up here. The continent's laid out so neatly.

My three friends and I ford creeks each day (full-fledged streams anyplace else), boots slung around our necks, barefoot if the bottom is smooth, or in running shoes if it's shalely. The green water is so astoundingly, miraculously cold that pain is a poor word for the sensation that penetrates our bones. Wonder or astonishment might be better. On the far banks we howl like wolves and lace our running shoes through a packstrap to let them dry. Once again I'm the last up the steep bank. I've found a wheatear's nest of twigs and grass in a cleft and inspect it. Then I, too, trudge up the caribou trail to the tussocks above the unnamed stream. The trail continues to climb, contours around a hillside and crosses a high ridge.

Shazam! Over the top the country makes good its billing. The Hulahula River loops in a wide valley below us, the Michaelson Glacier rises beyond, clouds cut off the summits of the mountains and beneath their silver-gray bottom are the tiny, grazing specks of Dall sheep.

Again everyone leaves before I do. I've taken off my pack; I shoot some pictures; I try to identify an unknown grass (unsuccessfully). Finally I take a last drink of water (a hydrated body is a healthy body!) and, having procrastinated as long as possible, shoulder my awesome pack.

A breeze has sprung up. I take a few steps across the tundra and become aware of a tinkling following me. The tinkling is so pure, delicate and fine, so angelic and graceful, that I stop, bemused, and turn around with the utmost care, fearful that I'll scare this sprite or new sort of hummingbird away. But there's nothing there.

I continue my 360° circle and the tinkling – laughing like the carefree voice of a 14-year-old girl – follows me, exactly behind my shoulders. Could it be that I've imagined this whole trip to Alaska and that I'm really someplace else? The tinkling – repeating a harp's pure C in liquid variation – must be from the Andes. Surely I'll make another circle and see Incan friends sitting by a terraced field and they'll wave. Or perhaps it's an Andean flute I'm hearing, and soon I'll spy a Peruvian shepherd, poncho blowing in the wind as he plays sweet songs to his llamas. But no shepherd appears. The Michaelson Massif, snow, granite and clouds, remains.

No, of course I'm not in Peru. Silly. I'm in Nepal. I've never left the Khumbu, the last three years have been a dream, and just down this trail I'll see a Buddhist chorten, its windchime singing from its gable. Or more likely, considering that there were no villages indicated on our map when I looked at it this morning, the tinkling I keep hearing must be a solitary yak herder shuffling along in his felt boots, his moustaches trailing on his chest while he spins his silver prayer wheel and mutters his chants.

Yes, I'm in the high country of Nepal, and the tinkling is the rapids of the Dudh Kosi River, a herder's prayer wheel, the bells of his yak and a chorten's windchime, all mingling together. Soon, from that ridgetop covered with rhododendron and pine, a monk will blow his 12-foot horn and its great soulful call – *om mani padme om*, behold the jewel in the lotus flower – will settle with the setting sun.

But no yak herder appears, no chorten stands down the trail, no monk blows his horn, and the sun will not dip below the horizon for another month. There is the ice of the Arctic Ocean, there the gray Hulahula River, and there and there and there, in every compass direction, the tundra – hundreds, thousands of miles of it, the Alaskan-Yukon-Northwest Territories hinterland, filled with migrating caribou, grizzlies, Dall sheep, very few people, and this mysterious tinkling. I'm losing my mind.

I close my eyes and concentrate. Then I reach behind me, touch my hand to a certain place on my pack and the tinkling stops. When I let go, it resumes, happy and trilling. The tips of my running shoes' laces, blown by the wind, have been playing chimes against the aluminum frame of my backpack.

Satisfied that my brain hasn't turned to oatmeal, I continue along the caribou trail to the Hulahula, the shoelaces playing their glee. But only a couple hundred feet down, as I drop out of the wind, the chimes fall silent. I stare at the Dall sheep across the valley, at the caribou prints beneath my boots, at the tundra's emptiness stretching far enough so that, for once in my life, I feel truly free.

Wondering if my companions are getting angry at my daily laggings, I walk backwards until I stand on the ridgetop again and the wind catches my laces and sets them to singing by my ear. Several minutes go by as I stand there, listening to the sort of music people make – on their high terraced hillsides, along their high mountain paths, with instruments lovingly crafted or only chanced upon. Then I hike down to the river, deep in the silent Alaskan wilderness.

Flying For 1002

Cleaning the Helio Courier's windshield is a rite of the morning. Don Ross, the assistant manager of the Arctic National Wildlife Refuge in northeastern Alaska, stands on the wheel strut of the orange and white, single engine plane and sprays a sweet smelling paste on the cockpit's plexiglass. The cold Arctic breeze flays the paper towel he rubs over the windows. Don has red hair, turning blond with age (he's almost 40), and an understated R.A.F. moustache. In another time his blue eyes would have searched for German fighters from the cockpit of a Spitfire. Now, a participant in the Department of the Interior's 1002 study, he helps spot grizzly bears, caribou, and musk ox in the foothills of the 19-million-acre refuge, a hunk of country the size of the state of Maine.

The 1002 study (everyone pronounces it "ten-oh-two"), was mandated by the Alaska National Interest Lands Conservation Act of 1980 (ANILCA), which in turn was birthed out of the Alaska Native Claims Settlement Act of 1971 (ANCSA). It is designed to investigate the sensitivity of the refuge's wildlife to projected oil drilling. Seismic exploration is taking place on the coastal plain of the refuge during the winters of 1984 to 1986. By September of 1986 the Secretary of the Interior must submit the data from both the geological and biological surveys to Congress, which will then have the unenviable task of deciding whether to allow further petroleum development in an area that has been called by one biologist of the U.S. Fish & Wildlife Service, "the most untouched and pristine coast left in northern Alaska."

So, hoping to demonstrate that the mammals, birds, and fish who live in the refuge might be adversely affected by the extensive industrial corridors that would usurp their home grounds, Don cleans his windshield, adjusts the tracking antennas on his wings, loads Larry Martin and Tom Wilners, the biological technicians, into his plane, squeezes me in the back (observer), and taxis down the gravel runway of Barter Island – home of a D.E.W. line station, the Inupiat village of Kaktovik, and the main scrambling strip for entry into ANWR, the United States' second biggest, least spoiled and, some feel, most endangered wild country. Everyone has a war.

We head inland at 3000 feet. The desolate, spiny mountains of the Brooks Range lie ahead, the ice of the Arctic Ocean retreats behind. Below, the shadow of our plane crosses the pale-green, muskrat-brown tundra. Water lies everywhere: six major rivers, hundreds of ponds, and a horizon-to-horizon sheen of bog. Odd that the north slope of Alaska is, in meteorologic terms, a semi-desert. Still, one must take into account that less than 10 inches of precipitation fall annually, collecting above the permafrost and producing the spongy terrain that is so difficult to walk or build on, the despair of backpackers and civil engineers alike. Ideal country for caribou, though, who travel across it effortlessly on their big splayed hooves and long legs, give birth on its barrenness, and eventually die here, leaving the occasional antler as a memento to a life that is an enduring fast.

The beeps begin as we fly over the foothills. Don loses altitude. Larry peers from the starboard window, squinting into the sun. Tom, next to me in the rear of the plane, bends over a topographic map and puts an X on an anonymous looking hillside. Circling – now the peaks of the Brooks Range off the wing, now the ice of the distant ocean – we search for the radio-collared bear.

"There it is!" Larry's voice crackles on the headphones.

We stare at the drainage to which he points and sweep our binoculars over the tundra. Don loses more altitude and suddenly we see two hamsters, one larger than the other, grazing slowly, heads lowered to the ground.

"Sow and cub," says Larry.

Tom marks the information.

It seems that one could reach out the plane window and pick up the two blond rodents in his palm. Grizzly bears? Lower we glide. Don throttles back and coasts along the hillside. When we're five hundred feet above the bears, the sow and cub flee. Now they look like bears, but still in miniature, toy-shop size. We pull out before they ever become *Ursus arctos*, the largest carnivore left on the good green earth.

We head west along the foothills, finding bears in every drainage, 22 in all. We see a pair of wolves, white and black, who run, tails between their legs, through the scrub willow at the approach of the plane, and soon thereafter a couple musk ox, their shaggy coats making them appear, from 1000 feet, like the caparisoned horses in a child's cavalry. Round about noon we cross into Canadian airspace, only to discover that the coastal plain of the Yukon looks no different from the coastal plain of Alaska. It's just as vast, just as flat, and just as marked by an endless repetitive series of polygons, created when the tundra freezes, cracks, and heaves upwards, giving the northern landscape a geometric and wrought appearance that would please a theist. It's also just as marked for development as the adjacent hinterlands of Alaska.

Dome Petroleum, Esso, and Gulf Canada have sunk exploratory wells in the Beaufort Sea, and Esso has proposed a pipeline to transport crude up the Mackenzie River Valley. Gulf, on the other hand, has proposed a harbor for Stokes Point on the north shore of the Yukon. Dome would also like to see a harbor on the coast and has eyed Kings Point, just south of Herschel Island. Here Peter Kiewit Sons Co. Ltd., a multinational firm based in the U.S., has proposed a quarry, using the rock to build artificial islands for drilling structures in the Beaufort Sea. The access road Kiewit would construct, as well as a proposed all-weather highway connecting Kings Point with the Dempster Highway, further to the south, would transect the migration of the Porcupine Caribou Herd.

Moreover, the Stokes port and quarry are within the boundaries of the 15,000-square-mile area of the northern Yukon that was withdrawn from appropriation in 1978 and which was designated for national park status in 1984. The delays in finalizing the park boundaries have stemmed from the unresolved land claims of the Inuvialuit (Eskimo) and Dene (Indian), and the lack of a comprehensive development package that would balance extracting energy resources with preserving a subsistence culture. The delays, however, have made industry impatient, and the result has been the far-reaching plans for the Yukon coast. Taken one by one, such developments could prove benign in their impact. But strung together into an interlocking web of arctic industrial centers and transportation corridors, they could seriously affect the free movements of the great herds of wild northern deer, according to Ken Whitten, a caribou biologist with the Alaska Department of Fish and Game. One of his colleagues and one of Alaska's most well-known caribou researchers, Ray Cameron, has also expressed concern over the long-range effects of extreme North Slope development. In a recent issue of *Arctic*, Cameron noted the "haphazard matrix of roads, pipelines and facilities" that have characterized the expansion of Prudhoe Bay and the consequent loss of caribou habitat that has occurred. If a large percentage of the Arctic Slope were developed in a similar unplanned manner, Cameron believes that the ". . . loss of access to favorable calving areas might . . . be catastrophic to calving caribou, their offspring . . . and, ultimately, to the herd itself." A third caribou biologist, the Canadian George Calef, has also found the prospect of development on the caribou's traditional calving grounds a threatening prospect. In *Caribou and the Barrenlands* he has written:

> At the time of birth cows are more wary than at any other season; they will flee if disturbed and try to lead their calves away, even before the young ones are dry and steady

on their feet. Any concentrated human activity on the calving grounds would interfere with the cow's all-important early maternal behaviour: cleaning the calf, nursing, and forming the vital cow-calf bond. If cows abandoned the traditional calving grounds for less favourable areas, fewer calves would survive. Therefore the calving grounds of all the herds should be made inviolable wildlife sanctuaries, off-limits to all industrial activity and transportation corridors.

Would that the world were so simple. Years have gone into the making of an international caribou treaty that must take into account the needs of animals, Native hunters, the state government of Alaska, the territorial government of the Yukon, and the federal governments of the U.S. and Canada. The treaty continues to be negotiated and the issues remain complex – so complex (and the stakes so high) that the Canadian Minister of Indian and Northern Affairs, John Munro, decided to temporarily reject both Gulf's and Peter Kiewit's proposals, pending the creation of a master development plan for the northern Yukon.*

If the caribou who annually cross this web of proposed industrial corridors only stayed put, everyone whose livelihood revolves around their habits might have an easier time. But the Porcupine Herd is as migratory as a flock of oceanic birds and has been since long before a neat international boundary was drawn down the 141st parallel.

The herd's journey begins in March as small bands of deer leave the forested valleys of the central Yukon and the country surrounding Arctic Village. Grouping together, they walk to the coastal plain of the northeastern Yukon and the Arctic National Wildlife Refuge. Here, free from predation by wolves as well as harassment by insects, which in late May still haven't hatched, the cows drop their calves and begin to graze on the new tundra shoots – a rich carpet of high quality nutrients that, in the case of the Arctic National Wildlife Refuge, lies over what has been

---

*In 1984 limited industrial activity was sanctioned within the boundaries of the new national park.

called by the *Oil & Gas Journal*, "Alaska's biggest known untapped structure," perhaps rivaling Prudhoe Bay in yield. By late July the caribou retrace their route to the Yukon and the mountains on the south side of the Brooks Range and there, pawing through the snow for lichens, spend a dark and ruminative winter, reflecting on whatever caribou reflect on while chewing their cuds.

Whether these northern deer (not to mention the grizzly bears, musk ox, wolves, swans, phalaropes, old squaw, arctic char, bowhead whales, seals, and polar bears who also make the north coast their home) can adapt to major changes on their home range as well as some of their southern cousins have – the white-tail deer, for instance – no biologist can yet say. And that's precisely what the 1002 study is designed to find out, with its radio collars on newborn calves, its hundreds of hours of air time (at $185 an hour), and its research camps spread across the coastal plain.

In the Helio we bank west, climb, and in the distance spy a helicopter over the ocean, making its way back to Barter Island. It's probably the boys from Western Geophysical, who have a weather port camp next to the D.E.W. line station. Outfitted with hot and cold running water, several thousand pounds of canned food and beer, and a library of video movies, they, too, are doing their bit of 1002. Come the winter of 1984, another exploration company, Geophysical Services, Inc., (GSI), a Dallas-based firm, will also be on the coastal plain, laying seismic line from caterpillar-drawn sled trains. Of the eight geophysical study proposals submitted to U.S. Fish & Wildlife, only this one was chosen by Keith Schreiner, regional director for the Service's Alaska region. His reasoning was based on public commentary, which stressed that, if the coastal plain must be explored, unnecessary duplication of the seismic work should be avoided. In addition, Schreiner felt that GSI's plan showed the highest degree of technical adequacy and environmental sensitivity.

Prudential as his reasoning was, his decision to allow any ground survey at all brought much criticism from the native, scientific, and environmental communities. Cat-trains have left their mark on tundra from the Mackenzie River to Barrow, and, despite the fact that the seismic crews of GSI will be monitored by Fish & Wildlife observers, many Alaskans, particularly those in the village of Kaktovik, felt that the refuge, a hilly region often blown clear of snow, will be permanently scarred. Although a less injurious helicopter seismic survey was proposed, it was rejected primarily because the data it would produce might not be as accurate as the information generated with ground techniques. However, not a few participants in the environmental impact hearings felt that the choice of a ground survey over a helicopter one sprang from Washington and not Anchorage and was born in the Department of the Interior's current leaning toward development. In short, if the coastal plain of ANWR were scarred by exploration, it would be a less likely candidate for protection and a more likely shoe-in for use as an energy resevoir when Congress makes its decision in 1986.

Even though the impacts of a ground survey may be of concern to recreationists in the rest of Alaska and Outside, few of these people will feel the results of the seismic exploration as keenly as the residents of Kaktovik who live off the animals of the refuge. Loren Ahlers, a former D.E.W. line worker and a resident of Kaktovik for 12 years, is one who uses the refuge often. Married to an Inupiat woman and the father of two children, he now supervises the Kaktovik powerhouse, water delivery, and sewage and trash pickup. A big man with dusty blond hair and blue eyes, Ahlers has a deep voice and a soft, self-effacing handshake. His house faces south toward the refuge and the Brooks Range, and looking in that direction from the warmth of his living room, he spoke of what the country meant to him. "I fish in there." He nodded to the south. "Hunt caribou, moose. . . . I camp in there. And now they're letting cat-trains in because the government has subsurface rights." Likening the federal government to a colonizing power, Ahlers concluded glumly, "We don't control our own destiny."

In a June 21, 1983 public hearing held in Kaktovik, Marilyn Akiak echoed Ahlers' sentiments and expressed what other villagers feel: "I don't know how the rest of Alaska is, but I know it's very cold, and the weather up here is very bad. I mean, you can go for days, be fogged in, or you can go for days being windblown. . . . Half the time these roads aren't open, and half the time the stores don't keep their shelves stocked. . . . Once you're out of something, you're just out of it. And we can't just hop on the car and run to the grocery store like you people can, go pick up a head of lettuce or a side of meat or a pound of bacon. . . . I mean, we have to sit here and wait, we have to wait for the weather. Our life revolves around the weather and the land . . . and . . . the animals."

Yet, some residents of Kaktovik find the prospect of oil development and its spinoffs not all that gloomy. Marx Sims, who has lived in the village for 20 years and has operated a hotel for backpackers, river runners, and now exploration crews, didn't testify against development at the public hearings. In fact, he is expanding his operations. Looking at the construction materials stacked between his family's home and the guest bunkhouse, he said, "Development is inevitable. So I'm gearing up for it. Television, electricity, heat," he continued, "have become a necessity. People need the jobs to pay for these developments. If the electricity goes off, people don't have wood stoves or gravity space heaters." A strong wind came off the ice of the Beaufort Sea and blew the fur-trimmed hood of Sims' parka. Jamming his hands into his pockets, he added, "As the youngsters get an education this'll become a city just like any other city, only with a different weather pattern."

A few days later, Archie Brower, the then mayor of Kaktovik, took a few minutes to push his chair away from his cluttered desk. Looking over his black spectacles and reflecting on the changes taking place across Barter Island, Brower said, "Even my kids hardly understand Eskimo."

The decline of Inupiat culture is sad to see, yet it didn't begin with seismic exploration. American whalers bringing firearms and alcohol to the Beaufort Sea in the 1890s, trader Tom Gordon who came to Barter Island in 1923, and the building of the D.E.W. Line System during the Cold War all played a role in drawing Eskimos into a cash economy and tying them to a worldwide culture. Since oil was discovered on the North Slope, the ties have become more enduring and the ways of subsistence hunting more difficult to follow. Certainly since June of 1983, the choices for the village of Kaktovik, once a fairly isolated community, have become more complex.

In that month the Arctic Slope Regional Corporation finalized a land swap with the Department of the Interior. ASRC surface rights in the Gates of the Arctic National Park were traded for subsurface rights on 92,160 acres of federal land in the refuge, the surface rights of which were owned by Kaktovik Inupiat Corporation. (Brower, acting as Kaktovik Corporation head and not as mayor, had given his provisional approval of the trade in an Anchorage meeting. No village forum was held and the trade was completed without the benefit of input from Kaktovik.) The expected happened. ASRC began negotiating with Chevron, USA, Inc. for lease and exploration rights, and their hope is to sink three wildcat wells by the winter of 1985.

Certainly everyone in Kaktovik stands to benefit if an oil facility is placed on the acreage in question. Yet the same block of land is often used by the Porcupine Caribou Herd for calving. Undoubtedly the herd will find another calving grounds, unless that land is also being used for petroleum development. We then are faced with the scenario described by the biologists Whitten, Cameron, and Calef: 140,000 caribou with no place to go, or at least no place that meets their unique nutritional and reproductive requirements. And so, like many of us who now meet the wilderness via the interface of technological assistance, the Inupiats find themselves in a double bind – how to extract one natural resource without destroying another. Sooner or later it's a question each of us must answer . . . or avoid.

After enjoying another half-hour of Maple Leaf skies, we cross back into Stars and Stripes country and drone westward to Barter Island where we sit on the ground, fogbound, for a day. When we're able to fly again, we head eastward – this time in a Beaver piloted by Patrick Valkenburg, a biologist at Alaska's Department of Fish & Game who is helping to photograph the post-calving aggregation of the Porcupine Herd. When we're about 90 miles out from Kaktovik, we notice that a fuzzy disease has appeared on the horizon. Spreading beneath us, it flows, congeals, and sends off long fingers of colony bacteria at a dizzying rate.

Patrick banks and descends. When he straightens the aircraft, we can see that the disease is composed of individual caribou – the Porcupine Herd itself, massed on the coastal plain near Beaufort Lagoon. Numbering close to 100,000 animals now, the aggregated herd of bulls, cows, and calves looks to be 10 miles broad and 10 long. Large parts of the herd graze peacefully; other groups, several thousand animals at a time, hurry toward the mountains or the sea. Wind waves of refracted light shimmer across the tundra and bend the legs of the deer so that they appear to swim through a translucent and rolling surf.

We circle and drink the view. We might be looking at a school of silversides through a scuba mask or the ghosts of a billion passenger pigeons. But we're not. We're looking at one of the largest herds of mammals left in North America, a herd that travels hundreds of miles across tundra and mountains while we to the south sit at our desks, work in factories, read newspapers. And yet, what is below remains a herd. It's impossible to imagine that there are individually bonded cows and calves down there, with distinct smells, voices, discomforts, pleasures, and deaths.

Patrick drops a little lower to give us a more intimate view. Now we can see tiny, three-week-old calves amidst the melee of adults. I try to pick out one calf and one cow and focus on them. But my attempt fails. The cow and calf I've singled out blend into those around them and are replaced by another and another seemingly identical cow and calf. I'm left with what Alaska always leaves me with when viewed from the air: the same white and black wolves, the same stolid musk ox, the same patient, rooting, and unremarkable bear. Yet confronted by the vast herd below, something not connected to the dry notebook and pen I hold in my hand, but lodged within my chest loses its footing, clutches, and stops. I'm carried east with the herd. Is there any person so civilized who would not go along?

We accompany their wanderings for only two days, photographing their aggregation on the windswept plain filled with marigolds and daisies. Then they head east with determination. And we return west to Kaktovik. As we climb from the airstrip and head toward the bank of fog on the horizon, the empty tundra still seems to vibrate with the passing of the deer. No one talks for a few minutes as we gaze out the windows at the last stragglers of the herd and the features of the coastal plain passing beneath us like a map: There the Arctic Ocean, there the Aichilik River, there the obvious line from the Mackenzie Delta to Prudhoe Bay where a pipeline and road may someday run, enabling many of us to get closer to the wilderness while inevitably chang-ing what we came to see.

Below, a small white spot catches my eye – again bacteria-like and inconsequential. Raising my binoculars, I focus on the white fleck and discover two swans nesting on the tundra, perfectly alone and at ease on the coastal plain of ANWR, birthed out of ANILCA, child of ANCSA, studied under 1002, another X among the many data bits, heading to Washington, far far away.

Places

Chores for half-an-hour now: first the long walk down to Alaska's Sheenjek River to fetch water; then the long walk back, across stones and through willows, the billy slopping water on my pants. I build a fire, fix oatmeal and tea. The sun still isn't above the ridge and feeling cold in only my shirt sleeves I fetch a pile jacket from the tent where the others sleep. I return to the fire and as I slip on my jacket, the nail of my index finger catches a long green thread, which emerges from my sleeve like a pennant.

The thread, I induce, is from my Nepali prayer flag (one of the four Bill gave each of us to carry through the Arctic for luck) and like the cloth it came from is as dry as Buddhist scrolls, as dry as Tibetan wind, as dry as the ancient ceiling beams of lamaseries, which have been darkened over centuries of juniper cooking fires and seem to store tales in their shadows. I rub the pale green thread between my fingers and think of Thamel, the name of the street in Kathmandu that ran down from our hotel to the market.

Along it were small grocery shops, selling red cans of New Zealand butter, dried soups, Swiss chocolate. And there were the butcher stalls, fly-covered yak meat hanging in the doors, the proprietors kneeling among blood and cleavers. The trekking stores were there, too, the bright blue ropes and orange tents bartered endlessly, some left it seemed from Hillary's time. Then came the Yes-Yes Restaurant where handsome, smiling Pasang served us Tibetan fried bread and dark Ceylon tea. After breakfast we walked to the market to shop among the narrow cobblestone streets, pushing our way, like everyone else, through the rickshaw drivers, the crowds, once an elephant. Horns tooted; water ran in the gutters; sacks of rice and dal lay along the curb with tins of honey, bins of raisins on which we brushed away the flies, baskets of watercress, bananas, and tomatoes. (We ate the vegetables peeled or washed in iodine for safety; but you got dysentery anyway and we cured you with amipicillin from our first aid kit. We were so self-sufficient, an expedition, you and I.) And there was the kerosene monger who became our friend. Sitting among his pots and barrels from dawn til dusk, he always had a cherry greeting for us as we came down with yet another Sigg bottle for him to fill. *Memsahib* he called you. Memsahib. Memsahib, remember how, on the way back to the hotel, we would stop at the Nanka Ding, eating stir-fried vegetables under the lantern light and sometimes having a bottle of Tibetan beer, which made us wish that we could go across the Nangpa-La and visit the Forbidden Land.

We saw enough, though, more than enough: 200 miles of trekking and climbing, a walk across eastern Nepal and all the way back to Kathmandhu . . . Thamel . . . the tailor with whom we had placed an order for a pair of yak wool coats. And the moment you touched the earth-brown collars, you began to cry.

At our hotel, lying under our sleeping bags, we held each other and tried to figure out how not to go home – that strange place somewhere under our feet and 12,000 miles around the globe where Nepal would be a slide show and two wool coats hanging in the front closet.

So we eked out the days – eating fried momos from the street vendors, buying trinkets and rugs, photographing every child who ran by us with his hoop and stick. Yes, we tried that as well:

putting away your diaphragm a few times and afterwards strolling hand-in-hand up to the golden roofs of Swayambhunath monastery where the monkeys yelled in the trees. And the light, most of all neither of us could let go of that light, shot through with marigolds and harvested wheat. You even put the orange flowers in your hair the clear day we rode our bikes up Nargakot Ridge to see the Himalaya a last time – white and hoving into the Asian wind like a giant flock of lammergeiers.

Some rain strikes my palm and I start, realizing that I'm along the Sheenjek River in Alaska, and you're far away with your own memories. Holding up my finger, I let my prayer flag's thread drift into the sky.

A Char
Heavy With Roe

O f all the world's gamefish perhaps one of the most admired and least caught is the Arctic Char. An anadromous fish inhabiting the remote high latitudes of North America, the char *(Salvelinus Alpinus)* is closely related to the eastern brook trout, though in breeding habits it mimics the salmon . . . with one important difference – it doesn't die in the act of reproduction but lives to swim back to the sea. A magnificent fighter when hooked on light tackle, the char often walks across the water on its tail. In the pan its meat is light, orange, and fruity. In fact, a fillet of char resembles a slice of cantaloupe more than it does seafood and leaves one wondering why creatures as physically nondescript as we should be allowed the privilege of eating such creatures as good tasting, beautiful, and peaceful as char.

We have walked for 27 days. We haven't crossed a road or a trail, nor have we heard an engine except that of the Cessna's, which dropped our resupply at the end of our first two weeks. We haven't heard another voice except our own, and of outside news – well, there have been the contrails of jetliners streaming over the Pole. But these have been more of the world of angels and not of this actual Alaska tundra world, interminably boggy under our leaky boots. Such a grand hiatus in the normal course of our lives (ski patrolman, geologist, carpenter, writer), such fistfuls of distance and time – 130 miles of hiking, 4 weeks of silence – gives a man (or a woman for that matter, would that we had a few) room to think, to carry a thought for hours, even days if necessary. Up here in the Arctic National Wildlife Refuge (or perhaps Arctic People Refuge might be just as good a name), there's enough country to walk in. There's no *Time* magazine; there's no "Today" show; gentility went by the boards a fortnight ago. We get hungry in old, old ways.

Halfway down the 100-mile-long Kongakut River, Will, the carpenter, spies some high white cliffs. He says, "Deep pools there, I bet." We all know what he doesn't add: there's likely to be char in the pools. After an hour's hike, we stand by the wide green holes swirling under limestone bluffs. The river's as deep as the swimming holes of our youth, but no tin cans or tires litter the bottom. Mother-of-pearl gravel lies neat as in a manicured aquarium; turquoise water foams and bubbles. Stacked one atop the other in this elixir are char, the biggest of them up front to get first shot at the swept-down food.

Having swum all the way from the Arctic Ocean to spawn, the fish are deep red around their gills and jaws. We can see this clearly when, occasionally, one of them rises to the surface and, with great delicacy and a quiet *ploop*, inhales a fly. Their backs are Appalachian green, like no plant in the Arctic ever looks, and their flanks are speckled with pink rosettes. Their tails are broad, their heads small; in the shallows, those ready to mate fan out beds in the sand.

We have carried with us for 130-odd miles of tundra, tussock, bog, and mountain a pack rod and reel that weighs 12½ ounces. Seeing as we have planned with great precision our daily meals of porridge, chapatis, couscous, rice, and bulghur, these 12½ ounces of rod and reel, light as they are, might seem superfluous to the nonfisherman. Naturally, they aren't. They're essential and pay homage to our roots. After all, long before Americans were farmers, they were scavengers of fresh meat – rabbits, partridges, and trout. Already tasting protein, we unpack the little pack rod. Will goes first but is unable to raise a char. I take over the pole and have an equal stint of luckless casting. Fredo (ski patrolman and the only one of us who has actually caught char, on a canoe trip in Labrador) suggests changing to a lure with more orange. Peter (geologist) has stationed himself on a front row sand bar with his camera.

I change tackle and on the third cast my line stops with no-nonsense finality. Hardly a moment to take a breath or even shout – the line slices downstream; the rod, gone slack for an instant, rebends; the tiny reel wails and thirty yards away the char surfaces and wallows. The line tests at four pounds and hums like a rubber band about to break. Immediately I decide that I'm going to lose this fish and, immediately, I decide to prevent it.

I cup the reel spool. I pump the rod and follow the fish downstream, taking the surges of its runs with a forgiving wrist and forearm so as to keep the line just below its breaking strength. I haven't caught a big river fish in a long time and I'm tremendously excited.

After ten minutes of give and take I have the char close to shore. I reach down and lift her by her jaw. Her sides are sea green and her belly yellow, flecked with shards of rose. She's 30 inches long and bulging with roe. I can feel her heavy maternal belly in my palms, as I keep her in the shallows while Peter catches one char and Will two, both of which are smaller than mine. When we ask Fredo if he'll not take a turn, he, the purist, says that he'll wait until the fly rod comes in with our next air resupply. So circumstantially, the other three fish released, the dinner hour drawing closer, Mr. Fredo unwilling to lend a hand to the larder, my char already there in the shallows, we decide to keep this female breeding fish for our meal.

With some reluctance, but with the communal good in mind, I bop her over the head with a rock and wince as my hand gets covered with blood from her gills. I look away – up at the sky – and imagine a meteor crashing into my skull. I walk downstream with the fish and fillet her, finding what I had expected: two long strips of orange roe, which I keep. The fillets weigh about 2½ pounds apiece and I lay them with reverence on a clean, flat rock. Then I walk further downsteam and throw the head and skeleton into the current, hoping that I'm far enough from camp so that the remains won't attract a bear. The head and skeleton sink away and I feel guilt swirl in my throat, as if I've committed a crime or, by some grave defect in my character, have let myself participate in needless waste.

Feeling low, kicking stones, I wander back to camp in a round-about way. On the white cliffs, I pause to watch William once again catching and releasing fish. In the clear water 30 feet below, I can see his lure begin its tawdry journey down the current. A char breaks formation, wiggles its tail aggressively, catches up to the lure and bites! A moment later – thunder after lightning – Bill rears back on the pole. Up on the cliff, I'm God. The char slams its head in the opposite direction – of course sinking the hook deeper – and begins to flail, roll, and swim frantically back to its place among its quietly finning companions.

Bill pulls it away and, contrary to what I expect, two of its neighbors swim quickly to its side and nudge it with their noses. When that fails to have an effect, they heave their flanks val-iantly against their struggling mate. When these efforts prove futile and Bill drags it further away, they abandon it to its fate.

I'm shocked and touched, and wonder what anger and lament I might hear from below if I had ears to hear. I descend, retrieve the fillets and roe, and carry them to camp where I turn them over to Fredo's culinary arts. He steams them with raisins. Peter, always one for a new treat, creates a wild cranberry sauce. Bill and I – the Asian duo – conspire on a curried rice. In an hour it's all gone into our bellies – roe included, though no one is crazy about the taste of the eggs. For the first time in 27 days I'm uncomfortably full. Yet, in a bacchanalian frame of mind, we eat some of the popcorn Fredo cooks and have a cup of cocoa with rum. "Let's pull out all the stops," he says, setting down his cocoa and heaping more driftwood on the fire. We sit with our feet to the coals until after midnight when the first stars appear, fol-lowed by a concertina of white northern lights.

Full, tired, content, I turn in, expecting to drift to sleep with the utmost satisfaction. But, when I close my eyes, I find myself drifting alongside the denuded bones of the char while other trout and salmon swim alongside and peer at me with liquid eyes. When the ghost fish fail to go away, I begin to think that, maybe next time, I'll approach the wild without my pack rod, that token of hunter-gatherism. Maybe I'll also trade in my guns. After all, an elk is bigger than a char and prey to almost as many emotions as a man. Many an autumn I have sent these fellows into oblivion. Yes, I say to myself, the next time I take a long trip I'll do it like John Muir and carry no more than a sack of flour and a bag of tea.

Then I recall the leather boots I wear (and John wore too), the gelatin emulsion of my Kodachrome film (made from cows' hooves), and the contrails that got me here, those vaporous ghosts of dinosaurs, narwhals, and baby terns covered with spilled oil.

Caught in the fruitless ontological web I've spun, I toss and turn myself to sleep. In the morning, bleary-eyed, I'm the last from the tents and also the last to leave camp. I take pains to see that it's spotlessly clean – the fire scar gone from the gravel bar, a tiny corner of a Band-Aid picked up, even the few twigs of kindling, that no one would notice, scattered. Penance. Then I sit awhile against my pack, hands around my shins, chin on my knees, staring at the pool where all except one female char still rise to the surface and inhale flies. But there's nothing I can do about that now, and when I think about it in the light of day, not much I would change.

I push myself to my feet and in one of those unbelievable but actual coincidences that stalk our days, I happen to crush a small bug as I stand. I can feel its liquid life spread over my palm, but when I look to see what else I've cast into the great beyond, there's not even an identifying appendage left, only a small red smear.

I snort, disgusted that, moved by the char, I'm also allowing myself to feel a twinge of guilt over this minute restructuring of the universe's organic matter – not even a chordate, probably not even conscious.

After wrestling on my pack, I hurry across the gravel bar and top the knoll above camp at a rapid clip. But there I have to stop and search a long time downvalley before spotting Fredo, Pete and Will, already tiny and, seen from such an Arctic distance, inconsequential.

The Sarcophagus
of a Cricket

A tarp, a sleeping bag, a few tins of sardines, and some pilot biscuits. Not what you'd call ample fare. Enough though for three days on the shore of the Arctic Ocean in July and an opportunity not to be missed: While flying with Walt Audi, Kaktovik's famous North Slope bush pilot, we spotted the leading edge of the Porcupine River Caribou Herd, bound for its winter home in the Yukon. We also saw a small group of musk ox, that shaggy relative to the goat, more woolly mammoth than modern-day mammal. Walt put the Super Cub down on a gravel bar close by the reindeer and while I photographed them for an hour he amused himself with my binoculars. Caribou stretched from horizon to horizon.

"I can't leave," I said when my hour was up.

He said, "I'd stay." And he handed me his survival food from under the pilot's seat. Then he taxied off the gravel bar and the red plane got swallowed by the Arctic sky.

Tripod over my shoulder, I walked among the caribou until almost midnight when the sun balanced on the polar ice north of my tarp. Weary, I crawled into my sleeping bag for a few minutes shut-eye. When I awoke, the sun was even with my right shoulder, dead east, and my watch said 6:00 AM. The caribou were gone. I jumped out of my bag. A few stragglers grazed on the western horizon, but the rest of the herd had vanished as cleanly as if the wind had blown them away.

Crouched by my tarp, I ate some pilot biscuits. Dry. I opened a tin of sardines and ate them as well. Oily. I walked to the Back River and placed the tin under water, weighted by rocks, so a wandering grizzly bear wouldn't find it before Walt returned for me. Then I drank some of the Back River, the water tasting like cold-nothing or maybe like a cold rock, except, when it got down to my stomach, it made my insides feel like they had been washed by a million showers. Refreshed, I picked up the tripod. Feeling unencumbered – no depressing newspaper headlines, no intruding breakfast music, no ploppety-plop-plop of the percolator to dull the sharpness of the breeze – I walked inland a half mile, into the scrub willow. As I had expected, I ran into the five musk ox, still chewing their cuds nearby where I had seen them from the air.

A fraternal bachelor group, each fellow a few inches smaller than the next, the five musk ox grazed in a gentlemanly line. When they moved, the biggest fellow led the way. Often they made deep rumbling sounds in their throats, expressing, I guess, pleasure in their forage. Slowly, I drew closer, until only 25 yards separated us. I took another step and crossed an invisible barrier. They stopped grazing and stared at me with lowered horns. I took a step closer. Suddenly the two largest bulls turned upon each other and butted heads with great agitation. Then they snorted and galloped off a few yards. I stayed put and their anxiety attack passed. From then on I remained outside the 25-yard limit. But, several hours later, in an incomprehensible gesture of aloofness, they simply walked across the river ice and continued westwards on the tundra. Within a few minutes, they slipped over the horizon in much the same direction as the last straggling caribou.

I walked back to my camp on the gravel bar and stood by the flapping tarp. To the north lay the ice of the Arctic Ocean, to the south, 70 miles distant, the mountains of the Brooks Range. In between, the tundra, the rapidly increasing wind, and me. Walt wouldn't be back for another 24 hours. What should I photographs? Flowers? The daisies, moss campion, gentian, and marigolds were out. Birds? A pair of arctic terns had a nest nearby. Ice crystals? Certainly there were plenty along the shore. But nothing called to me.

When faced with indecision, one can always butt heads with the next fellow in line; however, I was alone, and so I did the next best thing: I decided to have a cup of tea.

Billy in hand, I strolled across the gravel bars to the river and filled the pot in the current. The bars were covered by thousands of caribou tracks and on my way back to the tarp I took a roundabout way over them, picking up driftwood for the fire. As I knelt to break a branch from a tree, I found a pool left by the spring flood. One side of the pool had been sealed off by a clean wall of vertical rock, which formed a cistern about two feet deep. Though algae lined the bottom of the pool, the water remained as clear as alcohol. And in the very middle of the pool, not on the bottom, not caught along a wall, but in the very center of the water, floated a cricket, his back pale egg yolk in color and banded by three black stripes.

The rock, the pool, the bed of algae were perfectly proportioned for the insect – 1000 times his size and focusing all my attention on his miraculous suspension. A pharoah, lying in the sanctum of his pyramid, couldn't have wished for a more splendid end.

Yet I was puzzled. How had the cricket survived the spring floods, the crushing hooves of the caribou herds, and the wandering bears whose scats lined the riverbanks and who loved tasty little bugs for dessert? Had the cricket received a dispensation?

I couldn't resist asking. Using a slender branch of dead willow and without disturbing the water in the least, I fished him out and placed him on the end of my index finger. He had large black eyes circled by orange.

"Who did you pay off?" I asked.

The cricket said nothing, so I brought my eye closer to his, all the while balancing him just on the horizon line of the tundra. "You know," I said, "you've got only another spring before you'll be flooded away, or next summer, for sure, a caribou is going to step right in your puddle. Look at all these tracks."

The cricket stared back, handsome, leonine, and mute.

"Or just think," I continued, trying to get him to talk, "in three years they'll put an oil derrick, splat, right on top of you."

The cricket, maintaining his magisterial air, said nothing.

"Even if you make it through all that," I pressed on, "you'll just get spun off like the rest of us into the ether when the big bang comes along."

No reply.

So be it. I placed him on the surface of his crypt and watched as he floated down, tumbling one-and-a-half slow revolutions to settle on the algae with his legs in the air, as if grasping affectionately an invisible stem of grass.

"*Luego*," I said and gave him a wave.

At my tarp I built a driftwood blaze and placed the billy on the flames. While waiting for the water to boil, I went back to his pool with my camera. Knowing more than he, I took several frames for posterity.

Primrose Ridge

For the past two weeks, while photographing caribou, moose, and bear in Denali National Park, I've often driven under Primrose Ridge, a hangout for a large herd of *Ovis Canadensis dalli*, North America's only white sheep, named after the naturalist, William H. Dall. I haven't stopped. I have looked up, though, and measured how the Indian summer was burnishing the willow on the ridge's flanks from bright yellow to deep saffron. Finally, the fall decided that a week of glowing mauve would be the proper backdrop for these noble white sheep with golden horns and liquid, curious red eyes. Still I didn't go up. After all, Primrose Ridge has been the execution ground for so many fine calendar shots of sheep against brilliant flowers against crisp blue sky against jagged peaks that I thought, Why add to the reservoir of perfection?

At last September ended and the first winter storm covered the entire upper-half of Primrose Ridge with rime. White sheep, white snow, why not? I had to dig myself out of the tent in the dawn. I cooked some oatmeal and tea, loaded a pack. When I had driven to the turnout beneath the ridge, the sun had risen, and a cold wind blew the clouds clear of the Alaska Range to the south. Denali itself, grand white mountain, rose above all the lower peaks.

The 2000-foot climb was constant of grade and pleasant. My pack, about 20 pounds of tripod and lenses, was snug. I broke a sweat even though the wind was cold; soon I had to take off my hat and gloves. There comes a moment – many days out, companions gone, near a place you've wanted to see and have held off seeing – when you find your own speed. Having no one to wait for, I went faster; having no one to catch, I didn't feel pressed. Liking my deep breaths and the bite of my boots in the snow, I went quickly up to the sky.

Halfway to the top, I saw a small Dall sheep, staring at me from the ridgetop. A youngster, he had only black nubbins for horns. He made a slow turn and disappeared into a draw. I climbed into the gully where he had vanished and, after topping a shallow rise, spotted five more sheep his size, only a hundred yards ahead. They saw me and fled. Not wishing to scare them further, I angled away, wondering if I had ruined my chances. There was nothing to fear. After only a few more minutes of climbing, I saw three rams, their horns sweeping in full curls from ears to chin and back over the level of their eyes. Simultaneously, they looked up from their browse, spied me, and galloped off across a wide drainage. On the far side they stopped to look back. When they saw that I was only a man, and not a grizzly, they tried to affect a nonchalant air: one stared at the sky; one took a studious nibble of some willow buds; the third shook his head as if clearing his sinuses.

To save some face for them, I let matters be and made a long wayward approach, stopping occasionally to peer at the snow as if I had other business besides wanting to photograph them. Within fifteen minutes I managed to get a small esker between the sheep and myself. While concealed I put together my long lens, camera body, and tripod and hung another camera with a medium-length telephoto around my neck.

I wasn't quite done when I noticed a set of gold horns coming over the rise. One of the sheep had decided to investigate. He peered at me with large eyes the color of a warm low fire, then nibbled some willow. While he browsed, occasionally raising his head to keep an eye on me, I photographed him. Shortly he was joined by his two friends and they meandered up toward the ridge crest while I followed and shot.

Forty feet was about as close as they would allow me to approach. If I came only a step closer, they would raise their heads and stop chewing. Still, a 400 mm lens makes an object forty feet away appear five feet distant. I could count the rings on their horns and see the moist crescent of white iris in the corners of their eyes.

Wanting a few pictures with the falling-away landscape behind the sheep, I left my tripod standing by itself and walked off with the 200 mm lens to get a better vantage point. No sooner did I start photographing, however, then the three Dalls began to stare intently at my tripod. They couldn't take their eyes off it, and suddenly, nearly in unison, they snorted, wheeled, and fled. They ran over the ridge crest, not looking back once.

Amused at their skitterishness, and happy with the film I'd exposed, I packed my gear and wandered over the ridge in the opposite direction from the one the sheep had taken. It was time to leave them alone.

The higher I climbed, the more the tussocks and low scrub gave way to spires of red-brown rock. The spires were plastered with rime and the wind carried the sharp smell of lichen and minerals. It felt good to take long strides toward the approaching summit.

Almost at the top, I glanced east to where the ridge flattened into a plateau and there, loping across the deep snow, came a grizzly. His chest was dark brown, his hindquarters almost blond, and he crossed the roof of his world with a certainty and fearlessness impressive to behold. At last, I climbed over the ridgetop, looked into the Nenana River country to the north, and just caught a glimpse of a red fox dashing through the rocks beneath me. He had only just vanished from sight when an eagle flew slowly over my head, dipping slightly to inspect me. Perhaps only when these companions of the earth and sky are gone, and there remains to us silent glaciers, will we and the Canadians realize how graced we were.

I began to walk west, along the north side of the ridge. I hoped that, when I dropped onto the south side, I'd find the sheep again. Beneath my feet the stems of yellow grass had collected tiny spinnakers of snow on their leeward quarters like miniature sastrugi formations. I touched one, feeling it go to sleep for the winter.

When I crossed back into the sun, I saw the young rams I had spooked earlier in the morning. There were ten of them now, and I sat on a rock and watched them graze in their small basin while ice melted from the clefts in the rock behind me and broke sweetly on the ground. The tundra was a mottled rusty brown, and, as the white sheep walked over it, they formed a slow kaleidoscope of patterns: first a diamond, then an ellipse, last a cryptic mandala, the significance of which I couldn't appraise. Perhaps an observer from an older time might have likened the sheep's grazing and form-making to the shuttlecocks of the world weaving an ever-new generation into the changing tapestry of our planet, or perhaps someone younger than myself, watching the very same scene, might have said that the sheep were similar to the endlessly reemitted blips of a video screen – pulses born from someplace off the board, which pass quickly and vanish into another field. However, a witness far older than any of us, living in a time before machines formed the raw stuff of our metaphors, might simply have said, "I am *for* these sheep," using the small but highly flexible conjunction to imply the immense range of connections between the four-legged shapes making their way across the tundra and the two-legged shape sitting on the rock above them and slowly falling into shadow.

Within a few minutes it became too cold to remain seated. I crept downwind, around the feeding flock, and hid behind some boulders. When I lifted my head I saw a castle-like knob that had been hidden from my view before. It perched on the very edge of the ridge, overlooked the valley floor 2000 feet below, and on its topmost bench lay two yearling sheep and a full curl ram. They chewed their cuds steadily and looked directly at me, as if they had observed my whole secretive foray. Why hide?

I stood and very slowly walked directly toward them. The two young sheep let me get to within 50 yards before hopping off the knob. I ventured a few yards closer and the ram stood. Behind him a slate-gray ceiling of cloud hung over the Alaska Range.

From it three yellow shafts of light lanced onto the glaciers. I set up my tripod and big lens while the ram waited for me. Then he forced me to wait – he had a few more mouthsful of grass to crop. After chewing them, he turned his eyes on me and posed. I shot a few frames. As if on cue, he dramatically threw back his head until his horns touched his back, and he opened his mouth to laugh at the sky. Actually, he wasn't laughing but engaging in "lip-curl behavior," a practice which opens the nasal passages and enables the sheep's scent organs to operate with greater acuity. The behavior is most often seen around females in estrus, the males coming behind them and curling their lips for a better whiff. I didn't know whether to be flattered or alarmed. Nonetheless, with the shafts of sunlight pouring down in the backdrop and his head and lips thrown back, he made a majestic sight, whatever the cause. The film lever came up hard against the 36th frame, and he glanced at me with what seemed to be an amused little smile before walking off his perch.

Unseen by either of us, the clouds had crept up the back side of the ridge and now lowered, turning the world obscure and gray. Mist fell; I put on my hat, gloves, and parka; the ram didn't remark the change in weather. He continued to graze slowly into the basin that lay between his perch and the top of the ridge. Picking up my tripod, I followed.

The fog curled around me, now in waves, now in light veils, and born on the clouds were two-score sheep, mainly yearlings, though three full curl rams appeared on a shelf and gazed down at us. In slow motion, my every gesture as calm as theirs, I walked among them. One fledgling, his horns mere black dots, walked to within three feet of me, stretched his neck to the utmost, and stuck his nose, dilated with curiosity, close to my leg. His red and black eyes grew wide, but he wasn't afraid.

The clouds settled almost to the ground. I trained my camera on ghostly figures and shot. On the shelf above me, one of the three rams yawned, stretching his front legs before him and arching his back just like a cat. His ribs showed in his sides, his muzzle was grizzled, his penis erect. He took a pee and gave a nervous little shudder. One of his companions, in a playful mood, gave him a butt with his head and a nip to the rear. The old ram turned sharply; the other ram lowered his head and curled his lips, displaying a variation of lip-curl behavior called the "low-stretch," which indicates one ram trying to show dominance over another. Annoyed, but unwilling to push the matter, the old ram shook his head downwards twice, made a stiff turn, and settled back to his bed, laying his jaw on a stone and closing his eyes.

I took the film cannister from the camera, labeled it and dropped it into the exposed film bag. It was my last roll and I sat on my rock in the fog, watching the sheep move across the fellfields, the dark scimitars of their horns like the maidenheads of galleons appearing from the sea.

Suddenly and eerily, a strange and mystical call sounded from the clouds above us – "Kerleeloo, Kerleeloo, Kerleeloo" – accompanied by the flurry of large wings. I cocked my head. Yes, I knew the sound! Sandhill cranes were flying south over the Alaska Range, over the mountains of British Columbia to Idaho, to the Tetons, to rich pastures where the elk had begun to bugle and my friends were sharpening their skis for the coming winter. And the rams didn't once raise their heads to the haunting calls, didn't pause in their endless chewing that sounded like a glacier grinding rock into flour. The cranes continued to circle, wings rustling, their "Kerleeloos" plaintive in the mist as they searched for a night's roost. And still the rams did not give one upward glance, not one.

Sometimes the creatures of this planet baffle me. They have such grace, such beauty of form; they administer their intraspecie relationships with such polity and ritual. Yet, more often than not, they pass other species in silence, giving not a trace of recognition.

As I stared into the clouds, mist running off my parka, three young sheep walked by within *inches* of my knee. Startled, I stretched out my hand to touch their wet coats, but not wanting to scare them into flight I stopped my hand short. They continued to graze within a foot of me, nearly brushing my leg, and ever, ever, *ever* so slowly I stood without a noise. Their eyes rolled toward me, but they went on cropping the tundra, mechanically, diligently, filling their stomachs.

Perhaps the aloof relationships that occur between species aren't baffling at all, especially if you move slowly enough to see how animals react to other creatures that are slow-moving and non-threatening. If you create no threat you are accepted: you come to exist like sunshine and rain, like wind, fog, and the calls of passive, migratory cranes, which to other ears just happen to sound symphonies.

The dusk fell. The sheep became dull shapes. I packed my tripod and lenses, had a last cup of tea from my thermos. When the vacuum bottle was stowed and my pack on my shoulders, I said, *"Adios."* Not a head rose. Disappointed, yet not surprised, I added, *"Gracias."* I think the old ram on the ledge may have opened my eye, but otherwise the herd went on feeding as I hiked off through the clouds — one of that fated species who, needing to make a little spirit from matter, remains puzzled by the silence of it all.

Holy Bay, Or Another View Of It All

Glacier Bay. Muir's Bay. Holy Bay. The third, I think, sounds the best.

Almost a week now since the tour boat *Thunder Bay* left me and my inflatable canoe a few miles from the calving ice and a 75-mile paddle from the sea. Clanging, rumbling, and rattling – trailing a smudge of diesel smoke while the megaphone voice of the National Park naturalist crackled metallically over the death-gray water – the boat departed. The heartily waving sightseers at the rail grew smaller . . . tinier . . . teenier . . . vanished . . . and the *Thunder Bay* itself, a moment before as big as a planet (and just as secure) became no bigger than a coracle when sighted at the end of my extended thumb. Its disappearing act, however, was incomplete. A diesely throb sounded across the bay for many minutes until the boat slid finally behind a promontory. Then the tinkle of a nearby stream and the keening of the gulls reformed, as a soap bubble thrown misshapen from a ring steadies itself and floats peacefully toward the heaven.

During the week that has followed, I've received varied welcomes. The seals have been curious and wary, managing always to keep a bobbing piece of ice between themselves and my boat while inspecting my paddling style. The whales and porpoises, on the other hand, have been playful and interested, their sickle-shaped backs carving circles around the canoe. Thankfully (that doesn't give them enough credit) . . . considerately, not one of them has surfaced beneath my boat. The bird that has paid the most attention to me has been the black-legged kittiwake. Smaller than the common herring gull and with a sweeter voice, the kittiwakes have shown no fear and have hovered gracefully over my canoe while calling questions about my purposes. The semipalmated plovers with their stubby bills and white bellies have also paid housecalls, but in a very decent and proper English way—greeting me each morning by the tent door without hanging around for crumbs. As far as the glaciers go . . . well, they haven't recognized me in the least, calving off their bergs whether I've been dangerously close or safely far away. The mud too, the tide, and the rain have carried on as if I haven't been visiting. For the better I say. Who wants to be the eternal guest.

And now the muttering glaciers are finally up bay and the water beneath my 12½-foot inflatable canoe (a gray and blue craft propelled by a kayak paddle) is clear instead of clouded with glacial regurgitations. Streaming, lasagna-strips of kelp appear suddenly from the depths, unfurl lazily, and vanish as a current pulls them under. Sometimes I pick up a skein with one end of my paddle and flex its rubbery texture between my fingers. One variety, which lies wrinkled on the beaches, is precisely like the dulse I'm carrying in my foodbag, and I've thought it strange that I should have brought a half-pound of the stuff 3000 miles when I could have found it strewn around for the taking. If I had been truly attentive, maybe I wouldn't have had to leave home at all.

Certainly it would have been quieter. God! As I've paddled along, thousands of screaming, chortling birds have milled, swooped, skimmed, sauntered, and, yes, hurtled by. It's a circus out here and everyone's got an act. The gulls, terns, and kittiwakes are the saunterers, and though there's nothing wrong with a life of "leisure with dignity," as Cicero was fond of saying, I'm afraid to report that this clan has proven itself nothing more than freeloaders waiting for a handout. On an hourly basis their meal appears in the shape of a school of baitfish that has been herded by the currents and misfortune into small whirlpools off the headlands. The gull clan, scheming on the shore, flaps into the air with exultant cries and, wheeling and diving above the hapless baitfish, feasts. No doubt these birds are the resurrected loiterers who helped storm the Bastille, who marched on the Winter Palace that fateful Sunday, who were burned out of their Hoover camps, while the GNP sailed earthward like a goose with a broken wing. They're finally getting their just rewards—a perfect welfare state, the endless dole.

And if for some reason the dole proved intermittent or the rabble got out of hand, demanding free lunches without any effort, I'm sure the oyster catchers and guillemots would spring to the forefront and keep order. Black, sleek, aggressive birds, these are the politicians and press secretaries of Holy Bay. They squawk just as much as the gulls but never in a fun-loving, rabble-rousing way. Why their very flight leaves me shaking. Emitting high-pitched shrieks, they bank across my bow in menacing Vs and disappear over the horizon to settle an international crisis at the Pole.

Among all the avifauna of Holy Bay, only the puffins present a dignified countenance to tourists such as myself. They waddle on their cliffs, tending their young, or paddle serenely on the swells, fishing where they're most at home, their great Cyrano beaks giving them an air of sagacity. They inspire confidence. I'm sure when the world goes KABOOM and every one of us dive under our beds to clutch an icon or a gold trinket that we've set aside for a rainy day (not trusting even a bank in Zurich) one puffin will turn to another puffin, look down its long nose and say, "Hmmm."

All in all it's quite a place, this Holy Indenture of the southeast Alaska coast, this fountain of ice as Yosemite John rhapsodically called it, back when there were some real icy happenings going on. In the 100-odd years since his investigations, the glaciers have receded about 50 miles up bay and, if present trends continue, some of them won't be calving into salt water by the turn of the 21st century. But epochs come and go . . . come and go . . . and we have to be satisfied with what we have today: the Riggs, Muir, and McBride Glaciers, shadows of their former selves, and Mt. Fairweather and Mt. La Perouse still rising thousands of snowy feet against the western horizon. Not to mention the granite spires of Mt. Wright and Mt. Case, their lower flanks thick with alder, rimming the eastern shore. Flung between these two inspiring coasts, eyelevel from my little polyester bark, is an Aegean of islands with names like Leland, Sturgis, Garforth, and Marble. Sturdy, Normand, Anglo, Saxon titles. No Scillae and Charybdis here. No sir. No Sirens either and not a Cyclops in sight. How could there be? Tucked in my dry bag are both United States Geological Survey topographic maps *and* the National Oceanic and Atmospheric Administration's Nautical Chart #17319, "Alaska Glacier Bay." At this very moment, I could tell you that I'm 1.15 nautical miles north of Garforth Island, in 7 fathoms of water, heading at 142° magnetic, and at the rate I'm paddling I'll be at Garforth in 30-odd minutes.

But I'm not going to tell you such a thing, for I feel certain that my predicted arrival shan't happen, at least not soon. And not out of miscalculation. If the truth be known, and why shouldn't it be, the delay will occur out of plain old sloth. You see, my paddling, geared to rounding Muir Point in a stiff breeze, has slowed as the wind has fallen and the bay has grown calmer. I also have to confess that my dawdling is nothing new. I've done very little hard paddling on this trip, not much photography, and only a token bit of exploring. Instead I've just floated along, throwing in a stroke here and there to keep myself pointed in the right direction, all the while listening to the general frivolity around me. And I'm not about to change the pace.

In fact, to give you an idea of how things have deteriorated, the last few mornings I've woken up around eight, yes eight, and instead of leaping from the tent in righteous shame I've stretched my arms luxuriously over my head and reached across the folds of my sleeping bag for *Noble House* by James Clavell. One thousand three hundred seventy pages thick, it's the perfect book for such an undemanding holy bay. And before my former colleagues in the English Department of Colorado University raise their palms in disdain, and my hiking friends wonder why I'm not at least outside saluting the risen sun with the Surya Namaskar exercise, let me say, as a most unlikely but sincere defense of my reading this potboiler, that I can see only so many kittiwakes, calving glaciers, and diadems of wildflowers before the want of some plain old drama draws me to drink – a book that is.

The wilderness is great indeed, but when it comes to suspense it needs a course in basic playwriting. Why even one of its big scenes – a harbor seal getting munched by a killer whale – is over so fast that you only have to think about getting some popcorn and you've missed it. Yes, nature doesn't hold a candle to a good fat book and a clever guy like Mr. Ian Dunross, taking 1370 pages to slip through the traps of the KGB, the CIA, and the Mafia, not to mention the whims of the Hong Kong stock market, all the while saving (Hurrah!) the Noble House.

Clavell's no stylist (sigh) and if he has a moral message other than the "wiliest survive," it's escaped me. But he's kept me going, chapter after chapter, and the faint sound of the calling gulls, the waves, and the wind have been a perfect background, an ultimate MUSAC. In fact, after the first day of paddling, I became so engrossed in *Noble House* that I haven't so much as glanced at the Emerson and Muir I brought along, nor the Zen text, which fairly vibrates when my hand passes near its cover. Trying to read them out here would be looking at the Mona Lisa inside the Sistine Chapel while listening to the Missa Solemnis. More noisy places than this need such works.

Round about two I start paddling. Sun doesn't go down until midnight, so I can paddle ten hours and eat dinner by twilight just like at home. I'm such a creature of habit and, in a canoe, laziness. Dawdling, I paddle toward Garforth Island, the warm afternoon sun baking my shoulders and the bay holding me, a sacred child in its manger. Unable to stop myself, surrounded by mountains, sea and sky flinging peace and quiet everywhere, I bellow, startling a trailing kittiwake, "'Twas rehearsed by thee and me a billion years before this ocean rolled.'" And then, before the kittiwake can recover from its shock, my favorite Melville, "'Tis a mild, mild day and a mild looking sky.'" Yes, in about equally incongruous proportions, raucous gulls and noble puffins strut about this soul.

I spot two loons, their heads immersed as they search for fish. When they raise heads and spot me, the female edges away while the male paddles closer. He gives a questioning call, "Alalaloo?", and naturally I answer, "Alalaloo" (my best bird call, which has led not a few to make slanderous remarks about my personality). Hearing this giant floating log answer in an understandable tongue, the loon squiggles pleasurably and hollers back, "Alala-

loo." Five minutes of head-dunking, preening, and calling go by
before his mate, a fussy creature, dives out of sight and, by her
example, intimates that her vocal companion should do the
same.

He does and I'm left with the incessant chimes of his crazy
voice echoing from the heaven. And the bay, this great meniscus
reflecting the cumuloheads, answers a hosannah back to the sky.
A seal crashes its tail, hosannah! And I crash my paddle in answer, life! Yes, the planet sings today.

In my duffel I have yet another collection of these songs, which
I have taken the time to read: *News Of The Universe*, an anthology
of poems chosen and commented upon by Robert Bly. It's a very
inspirational text, as inspiring as the choir of this bay, and takes a
rather interesting look at how we compose and listen to our
planet's music. The volume first presents a summary of "The Old
Position," a time in which poets like Milton, Pope, and Arnold
wrote "man-centered" verse that separated them from nature. For
example, here's the opening of Arnold's famous tribute to aliena-
tion, "To Marguerite": "Yes; in the sea of life enisl'd,/With echoing
straits between us thrown,/Dotting the shoreless watery wild,/
We mortal millions live *alone*." (Certainly not here in Glacier
Bay.)

"The New Position," on the other hand, ended these Romantic
estrangements between men and women, men and men, and
most importantly between people and nature, to use the more
ungendered noun. Starting with the German poets Novalis,
Hölderlin, and Goethe, Bly tells us, and continuing through
Blake, Dickinson, Williams, Frost, Rilke, Snyder, Takahashi (to
name a few), and shamans of the Eskimo and Rumi cultures, it
presents a world in which people listen to the consciousness of
nature, as well as to their own, hence the book's subtitle, "poems
of twofold consciousness." As Novalis puts it: "The seat of the
soul is where the inner world and the outer world meet. Where
they overlap, it is in every point of the overlap." (Not unexpectedly, the lawmakers have just gotten around to instituting what
the poets have been telling us for years, the Civil Rights Act, the
Wilderness Bill, and the Equal Rights Amendment being legisla-
tive equivalents of the New Position.)

All this is fine stuff and most-needed. Only Bly's afterword, two commentaries which he calls "meditations," puzzled me quite a bit, for they sound the last note of the volume and indicate, contrary to what I had understood the book itself to mean, that the twofold consciousness is a basically sad one. Bly remarks: "The psychic tone of nature strikes many people as having some melancholy in it. The tone of nature is related to what human beings call 'grief,' what Lucretius called 'the tears of things,' what in Japanese poetry is called *mono no aware*, the slender sadness. Buddhists associate the 'slender sadness' with the incessant wheel of reproduction, going on without pause."* He also quotes a short poem by Goethe and comments: "The poem contains an experience many people have had: each time a human being's desire-energy leaves his body, and goes out into the hills or forest, the desire-energy whispers to the ear as it leaves: 'You know, one day you will die. . . .' When that whisper comes, it means that the tree-consciousness, the one in the wooded hill, and the one in the man, have spoken to each other. The human being grows sad then, knowing that he or she is an animal who will die."*

This is certainly one way to look at the planet, but I don't think it's a realistic way of understanding what goes on out here. Not only does this actual flying, chirping, squawking, broaching, spouting bay take issue with Bly's melancholia, but I also believe that he's made poor choices to support his theory that nature is filled with the 'tears of things' – the work of a Roman, a German, and the Japanese, urban men who found pleasure and a reflection of themselves in pastoral settings. If on the other hand, we look at a poet who has been close to the raw holy bays of the world, an Eskimo for instance, we might hear different strains:

> The great sea
> Has sent me adrift,
> It moves me as the weed in a great river,
> Earth and the great weather move me,
> Have carried me away,
> And move my inward parts with joy.

---

*Both quotes from *News of the Universe*, edited by Robert Bly. Copyright © 1980 by Robert Bly. Reprinted by permission of Sierra Club Books.

For the Eskimo shaman such dissolutions of the body into the sea, such recombinations of caribou and wolves, of seals and killer whales, seem as preordained as the crossings of comets and stars . . . and just as neutral.

Perhaps I'm being too hard on Bly for taking the short end of what I consider his book's long view. Or maybe the thunder of the glaciers, the chatter of the shorebirds and the smiles of the whales have helped to push my optimism about matters ontological into the realm of pollyanadom. Still, I can't help but feel that what is sad on planet earth is not the incessant wheel of reproduction and reassimilation going on, as Buddhists believe without pause, but those phenomena that brake the wheel in its full spin and actually suspend time: Clavell's novel for instance, or for that matter most novels, plays, poems and films in which one-of-a-kind people live their one-of-a-kind lives, get toppled short, and are celebrated, not for the great song into which they go, but for the brief song they trilled alone.

It's a grand fiction this storytelling business and, I think, a necessary one. Wasn't it Pliny the elder who said about the art, that it recounts things that never were so as to shed light on the things that always are? Where would we all be without our "never weres," our Starbucks and Ahabs, our Dunrosses and Bezukhovs, our Ophelias, Medeas and Scarlet O'Haras, our wonderful Blys with their literary imaginations, their exquisite curse which sees in most common flesh and bone, poignancy. Yes, where on earth would we be?

Right here, I guess, as good a holy bay as any. Lost in the rhythm of paddling, I float under the shadow of Garforth Island. In the quiet shore water, green as a forest's meadow, the two loons pop into sight again. The male, his red eye bright and cocky, his emerald head feathers flashing in the sun, spies me and instantly cries, "Alalaloo!" Before he can finish, my voice leaps in my throat. Without a backward thought I join him, "Alalaloo, alalaloo!"

Alder

While eating breakfast this morning in my camp on the shores of Glacier Bay, I glanced up and saw the snowy summit of Mt. Wright sharp against the sky. Its white ridges, granite spires, talus fields, and deep forests made my spoon pause between bowl and mouth. The sky had not a promise of cloud; Glacier Bay lay calm; it was a day to stir the soul to great undertakings. Step by step (leaping a bit here and there to maintain continuity), I visually traced the route from my beach camp, up the river emptying from the Dirt Glacier (actually quite sparkly), through a short ridge of alder (slow going there), and onto the tundra, the rock, the snow, and the summit five thousand feet above!

Yes, no question of reading this morning, or paddling further. A day for action and strong deeds. I put stones on my food bag, laced on my hiking boots, tied a windbreaker around my waist, and set off. The stream running from the Dirt Glacier came down to the sea through an alluvial fan, and on my side of its foaming channel a trail cut through the knee-high alder. Old moose prints lay among the bear scat. But not to worry. A silver police whistle hung around my neck. I gave a shrill blast as a test and a warning. "Shoo you bears!" I shouted (moose don't frighten me) and started up Mt. Wright, figuring that I'd be summiting-out by noon.

Everything went smashing for about 200 yards. Then the alder made a frontal attack. The individual, knee-high bushes, through which I'd been strolling, closed ranks, grew taller and more intertwined, and soon my trail became a tunnel . . . of sorts. Every which way the alder branches crossed and recrossed, their trunks rising six and seven from a spot like the petals of a rose. And those six or seven hugged in malicious comradery the six or seven trunks next door. If the trees had been as thorny as roses or devil's club, I might have turned back right away. Instead I pushed on, shoving and prying branches apart, the light growing cool, green, and silent. To my left I could hear the drone of the river, which was about the only sense of direction I had left. Mt. Wright, Glacier Bay, even the sky had disappeared. I stopped and came to grips with the situation. The river was my only chance. I bulled my way through the tangle toward the reassuring noise and surfaced above some small rapids.

Wonderful! I'd just hop boulders up the river and avoid the blasted alder. Wasn't that my original plan anyway? River highways! That's the way Alaska had been settled. It would be the way to climb Mt. Wright today. Hip-hop, jump-leap, a jeté or two and I was stuck. Deep foamy water lay ahead. The next boulder was 50 feet away. I waited, hoping inspiration would strike. It didn't. Wading through the waist deep water didn't appear to be a profitable or a sane course of action, and my only alternative proved to be a sly tiptoe crossstream where I gained the bank (grown much steeper), hauled myself up six feet of crumbling dirt, and was back in, you guessed it, the alder.

How a tree with such disorderly and jungly inclinations could have sprung from a genteel family like the *Betulaceae* is beyond me. Its second cousin is the hazel, or filbert, a demure and commercially valuable species, and its first cousin, its blood relative, is the renowned and quiet birch, a tree who, as even the most haphazard backcountry traveler knows, lives in well-spaced groves of dancing moptops resembling nothing so much as a circle of dryads twirling to tunes older than Pan himself. Birch bark has made Indian canoes, Norwegian roofs, Lapland cloaks, writing material, and tinder for campers the world over. Coleridge called birches the "ladies of the woods," and none other than the New England laureate gave an entire poem to this noble tree, saying, "One could do worse than be a swinger of birches."

Indeed. Once could be lost in the alders, the black sheep, the miscreant, the apostate of the birch family who, since Olympian times, has plagued the human race. Why when Phaethon took over Helios' chariot for a day, lost control of the powerful steeds, and had to be blown out of the sky by Jupiter like a rocket gone amuck, his sisters were turned into Alnuses for bewailing his death too much. You guessed it. *Alnus* is Latin for alder.

In all fairness, though, some *alni* are quite charming. The common alder of Europe, *Alnus glutinosa*, becomes a tall striking tree when planted on high, well-drained ground. It has a golden form, *A. glutinosa aurea*, whose leaves in autumn hang like rusted penitent gold. In the New World the red alder, *Alnus rubra*, grows up to 80-feet tall, and its hard wood is used extensively in the Pacific northwest for furniture. Its brother the white alder, a self-important but good-natured tree, grows nearly as large and with age produces a sagacious white bark much like the birch's.

But just let the European alder grow by some crooked little "beck," as they call streams in Yorkshire, instead of on high, well-drained ground, and it takes on every crippled bend of the water. Its trunk becomes warped, it juts out over the riffles in tortured angles, it twists and rises in agony toward the sky, dragging in confusion the trunks and branches of its neighbors. It becomes the stuff of nightmares, haunted forests, black knights, trolls.

Lest we North Americans were spared such horrors, the circumpolar alder made sure, as the last ice age retreated, to jump the Bering Strait. It gave Alaska a good dose of entanglement. Called "Sitka alder" (*Alnus Sinuata*) on the coast and "thinleaf alder" (*A. tenuifolia*) in the interior, this bantam-weight tree (large malignant bush might be more appropriate) so infested the water courses and lowlands of The Great Land that many a strong-willed pioneer fled with demented howls after trying to battle its green wall of perversity.

Stopping a moment and calming myself, I fondled one of its

branches. The leaves were slightly sticky and serrated, and a pod of incongruous, fleshy green cones lay in my hand. The alder has another claim to fame besides forming some of the densest thickets on the earth. It is the only broadleaf tree to produce cones. When all is said and done, however, producing cones is but a minor oddity in a heavy and mutinous bag of tricks. The alder's true perniciousness can't be appreciated until you push aside its boughs. Resiliently (perhaps one might say obdurately and even antisocially) they spring back with a lash and a snap. No other tree behaves in this manner. Bebb willow submits to being trampled upon with meekness. Gambel's oak knows when it's beaten by a stout vibram hiking boot and kowtows its head. Krummholz yields with a crackling geriatrical cry, and heather simply bows its head with Celtic grace and lifts its eyes only when one has passed. Alder does not yield. It catapults the hiker off the ground and flings him branch to branch as he tries to make headway. And it cackles in glee as he swims sideways as much as forward—precisely what I was now doing.

I dove. I clawed. I dragged myself down to groundlevel and began to crawl among the roots. What appeared to be a tunnel opened in front of me. I was able to crouch on my knees. I made some progress! And stopped. A lump of raspberry-red bear turd, not quite cool from the oven, steamed before me. I looked around, which wasn't very far. Alder leaves brushed my eyes in every direction. The whistle! Putting the bit between my teeth, I gave a loud blast. The alder absorbed my warning. I glanced at the whistle. On one side was engraved: Noble Metal Whistle—Japan. Without much confidence I gave another blast and shouted, "Shoo you bears!" My voice faded and there was a quiet, strong step—*thump*—several yards ahead. I sucked in a startled, frightened breath, my hand motionless by my mouth, one foot poised for flight. I waited . . . and wished. For a gun. A big gun. A 12-gauge sawed-off automatic shotgun. Or a .458 Winchester like the ones Alaskan guides carry. Or even a .44 magnum revolver, the sidearm of the Alaska State Troopers. Something, anything, besides this little tin whistle and the advice of the National Park Service: play dead. What I wished for most was some substantial firearm with a great big BOOM to put between me and the grizzly bear ahead in the alder. I parted the boughs and peered.

More boughs. I looked up. But the sky above, seen through the canopy of leaves, was like the surface of the sea viewed from 25 feet down in a coral reef. And up beyond that was Mt. Wright, the shining snowfields, the wind . . . only another four miles to go through the alder. I looked down. My legs and arms were scratched and except for my running shorts, T-shirt, and boots, I was naked.

Thump! But softer. Was the bear retreating? I leaned forward . . . listening . . . hoping. And my heart, beating fast, went out to my Neanderthal grandparents, slinking their scratched, terrified, half-naked way through the primeval forest. Oh, God! A quick bite in the neck and your last squeal wouldn't even make it past the next . . . alder.

Whump! *Crash*! Branches splintered! I crouched, reaching for my Swiss Army Knife. No time for heroics, son. I gave a blast on my whistle and fled, doing the Australian crawl through the alder. When I reached the river I jumped for a rock in the current and teetered there like a Victorian lady holding her skirts.

And nothing happened. Everything was just as I had left it: Mt. Wright's snowy summit still shone in the sun, its granite spires still rose majestically, and miles of alder still separated me from its heights. I pulled my chin. A hundred years ago, on the very spot I teetered, ice had covered the land. Fifty years ago, when the ice had retreated up bay, bare moraine had caught the wind. If I returned as an octogenarian, I would no doubt have the pleasure of strolling up to Mt. Wright through a diplomatic forest of tall hemlock and spruce, for the alder, that arch reforester, would shade the conifers' seedlings and bring about its own demise. Hurrah!

But unable to cool my heels for half a century, I made tracks, watery ones, down river. Cursing the demonic tree and casting wistful glances to the snowy heights I'd never visit, I tripped and slipped and jumped through the river and arrived at camp by noon . . . just about the time I had planned to set a triumphant foot atop Mt. Wright's summit.

What to do with the rest of the day? I looked up bay. I looked down bay. I looked across bay. For miles in every direction, in this no man's land between the glaciers and the rain forest, alder ruled. Damnation! I packed my duffel, loaded the boat, and shoved it hurriedly into the water. "You'll be gone in fifty years," I shouted back to the alder. And that impenetrable, irrefutable, stubborn green wall – said nothing. Nothing. I couldn't stand it. Taking my Swiss Army Knife, I rushed howling across the beach and chopped a sprig off the first tree in the phalanx.

A wind had sprung up, and it was a hard paddle rounding Muir Point. And the whole way, the alder sprig – which I had tied to my stern like a scalp – bobbed and waved and chortled a tribute to its clan.

Circumnavigating
A Dragonfly

Late afternoon . . . evening . . . sunset came go Glacier Bay: that time from about 6 PM until midnight when the water turns glassy, the light softens, and the mountains and forest begin to harmonize like a French horn and oboe that have decided to play a golden, six-hour finale to the day.

In the midst of this serenade I paddled along, two miles out from Garforth Island and two miles still to go before reaching Sturgis. And with no wind to fight, no seals to watch, no loons to call to, with nothing to think about except the possibility of my canoe springing a leak, which would drop me in the frigid water, I grew pensive and began to search for a message from Holy Bay to console my terminal imaginings.

If you want to know the truth, it's in this very way that most nature writers go about their business. In fact, it's our *modus operandi quotidianus*. When faced by beauty, boredom, or the big trip into the great beyond, we begin to snoop here and there for a hot tip, hoping, like players in the stock market, to buy low and ride some commonplace event into the blue chipdom of revelation, significance, or growth.

Annie Dillard and her frog-killing water beetle, Lewis Thomas and his Beethoven-singing thrush, Ed Abbey and Utah, John McPhee and "the country," and Peter Mathiessen and his snow leopard (which became a novel-long, bluechip message, though he never laid eyes on the Himalayan cat) are examples of buying into some cheap, overlooked natural stock, pouring in some capital (i.e., inventiveness), and coming out with a message full of spiritual, not to mention fiscal gain.

We don't have to look far to discover the roots of this method. That doyen of the nature writers, Loren Eiseley, gave us the primer in *The Unexpected Universe*. While walking the Gulf Coast and consulting the Standard and Poors of the sand, Eiseley found a shell imprinted with what appeared to be strange, golden hieroglyphs. He rescued the shell from the breakers and took it to a dealer who identified it as *Conus spurius atlanticus*, "otherwise known as the alphabet shell." Angry that the Latin name of his treasure meant "false," Eiseley refused an offer for it and, certain that it contained some still hidden meaning, kept it on his desk. While writing of the unseen powers in storm and sunshine, and how their cryptic voices are often misunderstood, he glanced at his old friend, the shell, and said, "Perhaps I would never have stumbled into so complete a revelation save that the shell was *Conus spurius*, carrying the appellation given it by one who had misread, most painfully misread, a true message from the universe. Each man deciphers from the ancient alphabets of nature only those secrets that his own deeps possess the power to endow with meaning. It had been so with Darwin and Thoreau. The golden alphabet, in whatever shape it chooses to reveal itself, is never spurious. From its inscrutable lettering is created man and all the streaming cloudland of his dreams."*

Nice stuff, nice stuff.

Unfortunately, I was too far offshore for shell hunting, and I hadn't seen my hosannah-singing loon since the previous day. Still you never know when a minke whale might spout a message or two right off the starboard bow, so I kept an eye peeled for anything southeastern Alaska might throw my way.

Sure enough, in a few minutes I spied an agitated scutter on the

---

*From *The Unexpected Universe* by Loren Eiseley. Reproduced by permission of Harcourt Brace Jovanovich, Inc.

water and paddled closer. It was a dragonfly, about four-inches long, brown, and in desperate straits. Wings sodden, going under, two miles from the nearest land, she looked as if her time were up. I thought of myself in a similar situation and without another second's hesitation made a firey paddle to her rescue. But as she heard me coming, she began to swim away, fear giving her new energy. Seeing that a direct approach would get us nowhere, I slowly extended my paddle. As she felt the blade come under her, she made a lunge to safety. I lifted her into the canoe and placed her on the duffel in the bow.

"You're quite the lucky dragonfly," I said.

The dragonfly said nothing. In fact, she kept her shoulders hunched as if she expected that I might swat her. Of course I had no intention of doing such a thing and ruining the karmic brownie points I had just accumulated. Watching my stock in the universe rising markedly, and not anywhere near the close of the trading day, I set off again for Sturgis Island, eager to set my charge on dry land with a flourish of noblesse oblige? . . . humility? . . . silence? I pondered what kind of message this was going to be. The dragonfly, oblivious to my plans, cowered on the duffel and shivered.

When my bow scraped the rocks, I said, "Here, we are, safe and sound." But before I could cup the dragonfly in my palms and loft her toward terra firma, I caught the scent of something sweet and luscious coming from the woods. I stepped into the shallow water, dragged the boat on the sand, and hesitated. Shouldn't I first send off the dragonfly? She cowered so timorously, though, that I thought it would be better to let her regain her composure. After securing the boat, I followed the heady scent past the highwater mark to a knoll on the very northern point of the island.

A more peaceful place couldn't be imagined. Calm water stretched toward a distant headland, separating the west and east arms of Glacier Bay. Up the east arm, from where I had paddled, lay Riggs Glacier. Up the west was Lituya Mountain and Mt. Fairweather, the sun hanging between their summits. Ravens cawed from the spruce and in the tidal flats beneath the knoll barnacles hissed and millions of orange-brown kelp bubbles sighed and settled. In the deeper water beyond, where the pink tints of the sky were reflected, flocks of old squaws, puffins, and guillemots cackled to each other.

Under my feet lay soft and giving moss, knee-high ferns, long stems of nodding rye, and proud fireweed. And the smell! I knelt and put my nose into the moss. Strawberries! Everywhere vines raced, their tendrils heavy with plump, red fruit. Untouched by bears, frost, wind, or the hand of greed, they lay asking to be picked. I obliged. I moved my mouth along the ground and slurped, strawberry juice dripping down my chin and onto my neck. I guess it was gluttonous, but consider my situation. As an experiment I had brought no sweets on this trip: no honey for my tea, no Tigers Milk Bars for a pick-me-up, no jam for the tahini, no raisins, no dates, no chocolate. Why such deprivation? Well, just because I have so much at home – Häagen-Dazs around the corner, Mr. Pizza down the block, peaches, pears, and o.j. in the frig. Sometimes it's easy to forget the miracle of infrequent nectar: wild strawberries; honeysuckle; this good green earth, holding us safe and clothed while we travel through the unmindful ether.

I ate as many strawberries as I could find, sat up, burped, (more bear than man), and wiped my mouth. Down the beach lay a black boulder, shaped like a tophat, which caught my attention. Having not much else to do, and knowing that my loosely tied boat would be safe on the falling tide, I strolled toward the hat. It was the strangest rock I had ever found. When I ran my hand over its surface, it crumbled instantly. Black as coal, speckled with flecks of mica, seemingly so obdurate, it had been beaten to dust by the sea and wasn't long for this world.

A cove opened behind the rock and another headland lay beyond. What about dinner? Phewey. Whose schedule was I keeping? I wandered above the jetsom line of driftwood and kelp and picked off a switch of grass for chewing. The old squaws, loons, guillemots, and gulls chatted quietly off the point. When they spotted me, they began to swim away – not straight into the bay but at a discreet angle to shore, paralleling my course down the beach, while ever widening the gap between us.

The beach turned south and stretched a flat half-mile ahead, its stones polished and so compacted that my feet sensed their first roadway in days. Eyes at my toes, I walked along, finding quick treasure: a convoluted shell, its upper half eaten away by the tide to reveal a nacreous interior; and a bone-white walrus tooth. The shell fit handily on my index finger and was as smooth as the sweet inside of someone who had recently sent me a love letter from home. The walrus tooth was no tooth at all. Rolling it over in my hand, I immediately saw that it was a tree root, polished, calcified and bleached by the sea until it resembled the molars found nearly a thousand miles away on the Chukchi Sea north of the Bering Strait. Roaming the hemisphere from a few footsteps, from a few bits of appropriately shaped calcium, I whistled and continued on. Not far. Giving a cry, I stooped and picked up a sea urchin, delicate as Chinese porcelain and perfectly sound. I had wanted one for years. Feeling wealthy beyond measure, I cradled my treasures in my palms and combed on.

The headlands rose before me — lovely headlands made of con-glomerates that had been metamorphosed into hornfels and schists. They were perfect for scrambling. Climbing the most difficult and interesting passages on the cliffs, I was forced to shift my booty from hand to hand. Just as I reached for an awk-ward hold, I heard a crunch and felt the sea urchin crumble against the walrus tooth. I mantled onto the ledge and looked at the shattered pieces left in my hand. Maybe I've always been too greedy. I opened my palm and let the remains of the sea urchin fall back to the sand.

The walking on top of the cliffs was flat and pleasant. Soon I dropped back onto the beach and within a few yards found a green plastic garden hose (three feet long) and the plastic lid of a Folger's coffee can. Wondering where all our plastic garbage is eventually going to go, I collected these treasures as well, aiming to stash them in my trash bag. I went across a little cove, squelched through a tidal flat, the kelp popping beneath my boots, climbed another small headland (everything was a perfect size for an evening's jaunt) and saw the end of my island. Across a 30-yard channel lay the rocky cliffs of South Sturgis Island, jag-ged as the spines on a stegosaurus' tail. The water in the channel looked deeper than I could wade, so I turned back. On impulse, I decided to return to my boat via the eastern side of the island, thus making a circumnavigation.

At the top of the next headland, in a small oval depression that ran down from the spruce forest, I discovered a pond. A few insects played on the surface and algae grew on the muddy bottom. But such life indicates potable water. I cupped a palmful to my mouth . . . and found it salty. I'd have a long paddle in the morning, before reaching fresh water on the mainland. Not to worry, though. I had two liters in the boat.

I clattered down a draw, the hemlocks looming cool above me, and waded across a cove whose shoreline was heavy with gleaming mussels. Pausing, I thought about picking a few handfuls for dinner, and, as I did, I heard an old ditty, "'It seems a shame,' the Walrus said, 'To play them such a trick . . .'" But wouldn't they taste good! I wavered, then imagined myself being dropped in boiling water. Shuddering, I left the mollusks alone and wondered why, in the joy of cooking's name, my level of gastronomic satisfaction had fallen over the years from cows to chickens to mussels, until lately only strawberries and their kind felt truly comfortable in my gut. But what if tomorrow or the next day, as I bent my mouth to some sweet smelling patch of fruit, I heard faint cries from what had been a thankfully silent world?

Ugh! Paying no attention to where I was walking, I tripped over a rock and nearly landed face down in the tidal muck. Backtracking, I found something the size of a dictionary, its side black and covered with barnacles, its top brown and imprinted with the claw prints of an ancient pterodactyl. The fossil itself was slightly larger than my palm. Thrilled with my find (though I knew that I was making up the entire story, and the print was nothing more than the happenstance of glacial striations), I pried the rock from its muddy bed. It would look wonderful on my hearth. Burdened now with a walrus tooth, a shell that reminded me of a blond-haired lady, a garden hose, a coffee-can lid, and this ten-pound rock, symbolic memento of a prehistoric bird, I splashed through the tidal flats.

On this side of Sturgis Island the cliffs were quite steep, their bottoms covered with orange kelp. I could either walk through the kelp or climb the headlands and fight the alder. There was a third choice as well. I could go into the spruce and hemlock forest and cross the center of the island. Neither of the latter two choices seemed as appealing as exploring the shoreline, with all its cast-up treasures and its promise of returning to where I had started without retracing my steps. I wanted to know the entirety of Sturgis Island's coast – one place at one moment in time. Immediately, I discarded the wish as nonsensical. Why at the very instant I had conceptualized it – while walking on the east side of the island – the old squaws, puffins, and gulls, that I still imagined to be cackling on the west side, could have flown away. Nonetheless, like a mapmaker copying a satellite's photograph of the recent past onto paper while the actual present inexorably altered his picture, I walked on, connecting every individual occurrence of my small circle around the island to the next so that I might hold the unholdable. An old wish.

Up to my ankles in kelp, pushing one foot carefully ahead of the other on a downsloping shelf beneath the cliffs, I felt extremely vulnerable. Might there not be some reptilian monster lurking in the slimy seaweed, ready to bite off my legs – some cross between a gila lizard and a leopard seal, still unknown to science? Relieved when I gained dry rock, and feeling foolish because of my relief, I climbed a fin of white stone, surprised an oyster catcher at the top (who flew away squawking in alarm) and was equally surprised to hear a sharp slap on the water followed by a hollow implosion. I never saw the seal.

I jumped onto the beach and kicked small stones along the tide line. There it lay. Another sea urchin. I was tempted to leave it. After all, if I really wanted it, I should discard everything else and bear this one precious object trouvé to my boat, wrap it in soft grass, and seal it in my water bottle for the long trip home. Then I, too, would have a treasure on my desk to read some winter evening. Greed and eclecticism prevailed. Jostling my other treasures in my arms, I made room for the *pièce de résistance*.

Only a few yards further along lay a tube of kelp. Eight feet long, pale as an intestine and faintly repulsive, it was thin at one end and thickened, at the other, into a bulb. It resembled a large white tapeworm and after giving it a nudge with my boot I let it lie. But why shouldn't I collect that too? Would it not be beautiful to a tapeworm, to another skein of kelp, to a pathologist, used to the anemic colors of diseased interiors? There is a bottom line through which even the most broadminded refuse to descend. I passed on the kelp.

Another seal slapped its tail and was gone before I could spy it. Ravens cawed. The faint mews of gulls came to my ears — I was approaching the north tip of the island. Within a few more steps, I saw the sun appear from behind the forest. The pleasant orange globe, so low on the horizon that I could look directly at it, had moved north past Mt. Fairweather and now hung above the great rocky headland, separating the east and west arms of Glacier Bay.

As I stood there, taking in all the good sunset ions, a blast of air rushed over my head and nearly knocked me off balance. I ducked and saw a bald eagle, white head cocked in my direction, glide past. It flapped its wings twice and landed in a spruce tree, where it preened itself before giving me a haughty stare. "Big deal," I called and marched on.

Then I spotted him — just his eyes swimming at the same speed I walked. The seal rose, periscope-like, his brown head and long whiskers glistening in the red sunlight. He came further out, almost to his waist, before sinking smoothly down as if pulled by a submarine captain below. He left three concentric rings, which faded into the lisping of the kelp. I turned an ear to the sound and tried to imprint it on my memory — that hiss almost indistinguishable from the one heard through radio telescopes.

Another seal followed me, disappearing as quietly as the first. Walking along and watching it vanish, I twisted my ankle between two rocks. Fighting for balance, juggling my booty, I heard the crunch of the sea urchin. I landed on my knees, opened my hands, and saw the splinters of the beautiful shell pressed against the coffee-can lid.

"You turd!" I shouted and reared back my arm to throw away the lid and the garden hose as well. But who would I be spiting? Fate? Destiny? Maybe we don't learn because we actually enjoy who we are.

I dropped the broken sea urchin onto the beach (more grist for the mill) and looked at the sun hanging over the northern mountains. Just then I recognized the knoll where I had begun my walk and, simultaneously, I caught the whiff of strawberries.

I strolled onto my little camp spot, placed my remaining treasure on a decaying log, and took a breath of innocent pride. After all, a circumnavigation is a circumnavigation, no matter how small the journey. I gazed fondly at my boat, that sturdy hypalon bark, which had taken me so far. The dragonfly! Her message! I rushed across the knoll, ran over the sand, and stopped before I reached my boat. Heaving a sigh of relief, I saw that my duffel, on which the dragonfly had ridden, was thankfully bare of any more pregnant cargo.

Ski mountaineering in the Rockies.

Home

In this mortal frame of mine which is made of a hundred bones and nine orifices there is something, and this something is called a wind-swept spirit for lack of a better name, for it is much like a thin drapery that is torn and swept away at the slightest stir of the wind. This something in me took to writing . . . years ago, merely to amuse itself at first, but finally making it its lifelong business. It must be admitted, however, that there were times when it sank into such dejection that it was almost ready to drop its pursuit, or again times when it was so puffed up with pride that it exulted in vain victories over the others. Indeed, ever since it began to write . . ., it has never found peace with itself, always wavering between doubts of one kind and another. At one time it wanted to gain security by entering the service of a court, and at another it wished to measure the depth of its ignorance by trying to be a scholar, but it was prevented from either because of its unquenchable love of poetry. The fact is, it knows no other art than the art of writing . . ., and therefore, it hangs on to it more or less blindly.

Bashō

From "The Records of a Travel-Worn Satchel" from Bashō: *The Narrow Road to the Deep North and Other Travel Sketches* translated by Nobuyuki Yuasa (Penguin Classics, 1966), p. 71, copyright © Nobuyuki Yuasa, 1966.

Entelechy

My run comes during the early evening, when the sky is veined with sleepy irises of purple and the air is lambent with the sounds of homeward-bound traffic. In the cool northern twilights, the smacks of balls, the padded thud of feet, are tender ministrations to my word-weary mind. Around eight-thirty, the light gone to pastel, I walk back to Devonshire, a residence of the University of Toronto that is situated between Ontario's Parliament and the playing fields of Whitney Hall. It's a good place to train for a first marathon. . . .

Cloudy back streets, a barber sitting in his chair, his shop empty. Saturday. Late. A ball rolls into the gutter, followed by children's shouts. Two women yelling. Yellow shafts of sunlight in the west.

The fifth mile. Hyde Park, the central lane. Fields slope away, I run through scattered maples and oaks. Two bicyclists far off, along the edges of a hill. My feet tap in the air. Squirrels perch in the twilight. A breeze comes off the lake.

Just Street, York Street. Couples going to taverns and shows, long gowns. "Why does he persist . . . purposeless." Words snatched from the wind. Up the hill of University Avenue, lights turn on. Cars and buildings begin to blur, the Parliament swirls. One mile to go. One mile. The grass is a bumpy mattress. I want to lie down. My right leg is in some sort of endless pain that crests and subsides, crests and subsides. A man in a gas station, sweeping water off the curb, yells at me as I go by. I turn Davenport, see the clock: I'm disappointed. One block farther, push it. One hour and three minutes. Eight miles and a bit more. Not very fast.

Strangely, I'm not out of breath. I walk to the house, put on a wool cap, a jacket. Walk. The lights glisten, are palpable. My vision is around me, behind me, stereoscopic. But next time, faster.

As I work at my desk I watch the rugby teams practice and the long distance runners, arms swinging loosely, slide under the arch of the great gymnasium clock. Small scale in the distance, the marathoners circle the rugby players, lap the Parliament, do it again, then angle toward Hyde Park, three miles from the university. A soothing view.

When not looking out my windows I've grown acquainted with some new words. One is frog, the deprecative term for a French Canadian. Another is ululation, which is how wolves sounded to an Arctic explorer. A third is *entelecheia*. It was left undefined by the philosopher who used it, and I went first to the dictionary, then to the encyclopedia, which had this to say: "Aristotle's term for that which realizes or makes actual what is otherwise merely potential." A piquant thought for a long-distance runner.

On the paths of the university grounds I've met other marathoners and they've invited me to the stadium to train. One of the men who habitually uses the track is John. A short, weathered Englishman, he wears green trunks, shabby shoes and has absolutely no flesh on him. He runs quite fast.

John's normal day is forty-five laps or eleven and one-quarter miles around the cinder track. Last week I tried to keep up with him. I made sixteen laps. Today we began with a mild 7:30 mile, then increased the pace to seven minutes . . .

It's raining and the milers are lapping us, yelling "TRACK!" as they dash by, spikes flying. On the field the football team is throwing down-and-out patterns; hurdlers, sprinters, and discus throwers are practicing – lots of activity in the stadium. It doesn't distract from the dull ache in my side.

At three miles we're down to 6:35. I feel lousy but decide to go at least one more mile, to match the best I've done with John.

It's raining hard, blowing on the backstretches; we're buffeted about. At four miles I feel slightly better, as if my body simply had to accustom itself to the pace. At six miles I know I'm going to make eight, maybe ten, because I feel so incredibly fine – no pain, my arms and legs working at the same speed as John's. I glance down; my thighs are covered with cinders from his spraying shoes. It continues to rain, we're soaked. John is in a red slicker with the hood up; I'm in a T-shirt; François, behind me, is in a tank top. I can hear his breath and his spikes.

It's nine miles and we've been running these mean 6:20s and 6:15s, John hauling on the backstretches. Head lowered against the wind, arms pumping, he calls, "Keep the pace."

I watch my legs striding and try to forget how empty I feel: just breath where there used to be muscle.

Then the ninth mile is done and it's nine laps to go. As I suck bellyfuls of breath, I wonder how to count the laps. Come on deep breaths, don't let John get ahead of you. I catch him again, right on his tail and think, Should I count one lap, then have just two miles to go? or do a mile and then have five laps to survive? The sound of feet on cinders, feet on cinders, stride stride stride, endless crunch. We're doing laps that are giving us 6:10 miles, and I'm starting to panic. Slow the breathing down: bellybreaths, yogabreaths. Calmness returns, and I think about how to count these laps and think about it so long, wavering in my indecision, pain lodged under my right ribs and rain streaming down my face, the cinders crunching, that suddenly there are only two laps to go.

We do a quarter, go past the block that says *fini*, and it's one lap left. The three of us all alone out there under the rain, everyone else gone for the day. I yell, "This is the forty-fifth, right?"

"The beginning of it," John calls back.

Out of the first turn I pass him, François right behind me. Doggedly John hangs alongside of us. With 220 left, we pull around the bend together, the three of us in line, arms and legs whirling, cinders crackling, full tilt toward *fini*. Eleven and one-quarter.

I put on a sweat suit, walk up the track and into the locker room. I undress slowly, then join the others in the shower. As the water cascades over me, I shake my head in astonishment: Eleven and one-quarter with John.

An interim period this, a hiatus between ambitions. It's nice to jog in the rain – my feet making squeegee sounds, my reflection a runny watercolor in the building glass – and think about everything. Mulched earth, hissing tires, the wind pushes softly. Legs cold red, shirt plastered to me; steam wisps from my shoulders. A ductile sensation this, moving between the pellets of rain.

The night comes. How long have I been running? Twelve, thirteen miles? Something like that. Figure it out when you get back. It'll be around fifteen. The car lights are a yellow river, a band of red squadrons. The traffic signals popsicles of green above them. Lampposts become star streaks upon the emulsion of my eyes. I squint – lasers pour through my lashes, eggyolk and emerald bars, wet spectrum. Tears fly from my face and join the rain. Two hard slabs, my feet turn a corner and slide from beneath me; my hand touches the asphalt, steadies; the legs never pause. Hysterical trees, furies, wave their arms against the sky. I bound up Devonshire's steps and the corridor light hits me like an electrocution.

Toward the end of the summer now and I'm doing sixty miles a week. After running 440 intervals with François, I hobble. The room smells of liniment and soap, apples and tamari. Leaning back in the hard chair, a book in hand, feet upon the desk, I look south toward Lake Erie, south to Colorado and home. Soon. Mentally I feel spacious, rested; my body is a seashell through which my lymph purls. Strong like a ship's sail, strong like a straight-backed, frail pioneer woman, I float through the people-serried dusk . . .

The city's going home to relax. I see it on their faces that seem to say: quick, escape, bustle to the suburbs; sigh in relief as the door closes, sealing them out – the miserable throng. A drink, dinner, quick. Quick, stuff it down, so that the dreamy anaesthesia will come.

Lightly weaving through the milling crowds, I catch scents of broiling steak, sudsy beer, tomato sauce, oregano, bad grease, and Balkan Sobranie pipe smoke emerging from a tobacconist. Canoe aftershave, car exhaust, menstruation – she gives me a smile as we wait at the 'don't walk' sign. I run on.

Up the rich hills, treed streets, Toronto below. Back again, Parliament. I jump lines of tulips, chase a borzoi. She chases me. Maniacal dervishes, we sprint inst and outst and amongst the trees until, panting in glee, she runs to her master in drag. Through the back gardens of the Royal Museum; placid statues, heads bent in the dusk, let negligent tunics slip from their shoulders. Grecian eyes, shy and proud. Past Trinity Chapel, the smell of incense. Around the rugby fields, seven minutes to go. Not a distance, but a time run tonight: run for two hours. Why? Why work eight hours a day? Why five days a week? We are the mensural animal.

I go through courtyards, mews, leg it onto the quad behind the gymnasium clock. Physics and chemistry buildings surround it. It's the cerebrum of the university. Around Parliament again, very quickly. The clock says that I've run three minutes too much. I keep going. It feels too good to stop. Around the block, outside the science buildings this time, back through the far gate. I see the clock again. Ten minutes too long. Stop. No. Faster.

Stop. No.
Stop. No.
Stop. No.
Faster.

It feels so fine. I can run forever. No pain, just calm breath. The breath in every artery. Supercharged, it burgeons into my veins – they're red as well. The edges of me dissolve. Particulate, blushing, I streak through the dusk.

Stop. No.

I'll run to Chibougamau. I've always wanted to see that town with such a Quebeçois name. It's only four hundred miles away. I'll run to Yellowknife. I wonder if they have a big yellow knife sticking in a stone in the middle of the town square. It's only two thousand miles away.

Stop. No.

Faster.

You have to stop. Everything stops. Even horses stop.

No they don't. They run forever over the plains, tails streaming. In time to my strides, I chant the Greek word for horse, *Alago, alago*. I am a horse, *hippos*, an eohippus cantering across the Eocene savannas. Primal dusk, plasmic sea, epidermal gates flung wide, we mingle—blood, breath, and air.

Stop. No!

Stop. No! For what? To do what? What else matters? Dinner. How can you feed the wind?

I'll make you stop.

Faster. Faster . . . Faster.

Breath. Nothing but rasping breath. Rasping, rasping. Faaaster . . . Ears dull, arms heavy, legs lead. Arms? Legs? They're back. It's back—the construct. And a madly beating heart, dry throat. Legs that were molecules of air slow. Slowing . . . I jog it off.

I wiggle my head, swim my arms, look at the twilit sky—beauteous night, sweet green smell. I do a forward roll and continue my jog toward Devonshire.

After stretching I stand on the scale. I've lost five pounds during the run. Glancing up, I see myself in the mirror. Tilt my head to the side, a slight bend at the waist, hip outthrust, slightly theatrical. *Rectus femoris, gluteus medius, rector abdominis, intercostalis*—tense, statuesque, calm, a museum piece.

I shower, dress in white muslin pants, a white muslin shirt; very cool. I walk barefoot, south from Devonshire, through cement neighborhoods, pawnshops, antiquerries. On a cross-street, a few blocks from the tall, vacant business district, is David's Beggar's Banquet.

A narrow easeful restaurant, it seats at most twenty-five people at hardwood tables. The walls display charcoal sketches, lithographs, tapestries. Fragrant oil lamps shed pools of light and seated on a small platform in the large front window, the night sky behind him, Jim plays a Spanish guitar.

It's late, there are few people left. I sit at a table by myself. In a while David comes out of the kitchen. He has a flaxen beard and a baldspot; long yellow hair falls from it and flanks his sensuous mouth. He has spent years traveling in South America, Asia, and Africa and, in this backwater neighborhood, cooks the food he ate during his journeys.

He brings me humus and pita bread, a bowl of carrot and beet salad, lemon the dressing. A tiny piece of goat cheese, alone on a tiny saucer. Then a pungent tea in a stodgy crock. The dinner is a Japanese painting, and my run a black stroke on the day's scroll.

Bakin Bread

Stress is all around us. A while back *Time* even did a feature on it. The story made the cover – a man's screaming head exploding out of a concrete block. In the piece itself we were told that stress is an affliction of the latter part of the 20th century, and that to combat it we could meditate, exercise, participate more in our communities, and reach out to touch our families. There was even a stress test by which, after answering certain questions and grading them on a scale of 1 to 5, you, too, could tell if you were a candidate for a stress-related end, particularly a myocardial infarction, i.e. – a heart attack.

The article made interesting reading, especially for those of us in the outdoor recreation industry, who can see stress growing in what, two decades ago, was a happy-go-lucky pastime. The reasons for this unhealthy trend aren't obscure. Media being what it is, and advertising being what it is even more so (pushy, intrusive, manipulative), all of us must now share the outdoors with the champion recreators media and advertising have created. These people, often in the pay of one or more segments of the outdoor industry, travel the planet, running faster footraces, floating wilder rivers, climbing harder mountains, sailing seas in ever smaller and/or faster boats, and bicycling where bikes have never gone before. Some of these folks have turned even such mindless pursuits as Frisbee and Hacky-Sac into world-class events.

Naturally, all of us want to make a living at what we enjoy doing, and so we write guide books about the places in which we've climbed, give testimonials about the gear on which we've skied, and churn out monthly columns about whatever it is we do best. Soon, locked into our lecture and business schedules, we do less of what we love and have more stress. And the only way to gain more free time to go to more exotic places is to do more consulting and more freelancing, which only closes the circle tighter and digs the hole deeper. The way in which the 13th century had its Black Plague and the poor gallant men on the Marne had their mustard gas, we, too, have an environmental hazard that's going to get us. Maybe, rather than calling it stress, which is a result more than a condition, we should name our particular hazard *overloads*.

They affect us not only in our work, but in experience itself. For instance, with all forms of recreation so blatantly popularized, we have come to see the evaporation of the private niche. In short, there is nowhere to get away from the records – the fastest 10K, the highest oxygenless ascent, the longest time to stay upright on a bicycle without going anywhere – and just enjoy oneself at a nice, slow, personal pace.

The price that all participants in sports pay for this constant heralding of world, national, and gender records is a certain mass feeling of never having arrived and, worse, the depressing sensation that one will never catch up to a record that recedes like a rocket going into orbit.

The antidote for this malaise seems simple enough, though. We should participate only in activities that don't change their records on a weekly basis. Sad to say, finding such a sport has baffled the keenest minds, and with good reason. Technology speeds exchange geometrically and has eroded first our records then our anchorages, which once supported entire societies. For example, remote wilderness landscapes change yearly as more of us want to see them before others ruin them. As divorce has become easier and life longer, our parents remarry and have second families; we, as well, become partners to several spouses and breed children who live with adults not biologically related to them. "Family" can mean as much as "sugar" and "cream" in a world where sorbitol and whitener are found regularly on tables. Faced with these changes, some may cast onto religious faith as a fundamental, ongoing value – something above sport and its records, more enduring than landscape, a supra-family and shield. But in a world where we all have had to learn to adapt quickly to survive, those faiths that don't grow with the times are looked at with skepticism. On the other hand, those that change with every season are immediately part and parcel of what we're trying to cure. We reject them as spineless. Poor faith, there's no middle ground for it. What we really need is a solid meter rod, one that will measure the same length again and again, but not hit us over the head with anything too spiritual.

Well, I've discovered one. It's the jar of sourdough starter in my refrigerator. The jar is neither old, charming, nor valuable. In fact, it's a plastic wheat germ container, a brand long since discontinued. Holding about six cups, it's coldproof, shatterproof, airtight, corrosion resistant, chemically inert, and has stored my starter for the past four years. It's the perfect eternity chamber.

The starter it holds was made from fermented potatoes and, at this writing, has birthed hundreds of loaves of bread, not to mention English muffins, flapjacks, and chapatis. It has outlived the marriage to which it contributed the nuptial bread, it has moved to four different homes, and the loaves it has produced, though having their individual ups and downs, have remained remarkably and satisfyingly consistent. This may have a little to do with how the bread is put together . . . "put together" being a nice neutral term, rather than "created," which smacks of a biblical sect, or "fabricated," full as it is of industrial overtones.

Anyhow, when I've been away a few weeks, hot on the experience trail, nearly the first thing I do when I come home is put together some bread. This happens in the following way. I pour the separated starter – its top two inches a horrible-looking black liquid, its bottom a doughy sludge – into a large bowl. I then add whole wheat flour, followed by water. After mixing this into a muddy "sponge," I place the bowl in a warm place for the night.

When the bowl is uncovered in the morning, the starter, bubbling excitedly, releases a pungent, sour smell throughout the kitchen. This gas is the exhaled breath of millions of awakened sourdough bacteria. I refill the wheat germ container with several cups of sponge (in effect, the sponge has become a large batch of starter) and put my time capsule in the frig. I add oil, salt, and more flour to what I have left in the bowl, and when I can't stir this mixture any more, I drop what is now dough onto a floured board. Almost always this "putting together" takes place in the early morning, when the house is quiet. Snow might be falling, or the sun might be edging through the leaves that line my kitchen window.

Legs spread for stability, I rock the dough back and forth on the board, getting my whole body into the motion. I spread the dough and reform it – roll it, work my knuckles through it, add more flour until it is elastic and firm, manageable yet moist, a large chunk of living protoplasm that I can feel breathing between my hands.

While kneading my sourdough bread, I don't believe I think of my technique, for the pastime of putting together bread doesn't demand the sort of concentration that rock climbing, skiing, or kayaking does. And since there's never been a grading system for kneading bread, no 5.10 or WWIV, and not even a Guiness Book record for the fastest time to make five pounds of water and flour into dough, the activity of kneading immediately removes two of the leading perpetrators of stress: competition and performance. True, some recipe books such as the *Tasahara*, a serene and helpful guide, recommend kneading dough at least 200 times. Years ago, when I first began bakin bread, I followed these instructions. Now, I couldn't tell you if I knead my bread 50 or 1000 times. I'm sure that I've touched the two extemes. And since I've already baked the best possible bread in the world, on about three occasions, I can't hope to better my performance and so have nothing to strive for except putting together a yeoman-like loaf: nutritious, tangy on the tongue, sliceable with a sharp knife, durable in my backpack, and with a decent shelf life. I have to admit, though, with all due modesty, that shelf life has never been a problem with my bread. Like the athlete dying young, it is usually consumed grandly in its prime.

And all this – the putting together, the eating, the contentment that follows – seem both useful and good. However, now and then, when putting together sourdough seems too lengthy, I have moments of doubt. As I shop in the supermarket between the airport and home, knowing full well that an empty frig will greet me, I pause at the bread shelves and heft one of the "health" selections. A grand loaf to be sure. Just read the ingredients: whole wheat flour, soy flour, graham flour, raisins, sunflower seeds, safflower oil, honey . . ." On and on goes the list. I bring the loaf close to my nose. The smell is delicious, and I know the taste will be similar. What's more, I'd have toast in the morning instead of a bowl of bubbling sourdough starter, hours away from its finished form.

Still, most days, I return the well-wrought loaf to the shelf. In the end, or rather, in the beginning, it comes down to the putting together. Alone in the silent morning house – the radio off, the telephone unplugged, the cat purring figure-eights around my ankles while I rock back and forth, wrist deep in dough – I know what He knew along the first river, working with dedication and without hurry, for an audience of one.

Water Dreams
In The Desert

Four shades of green rise from the muddy Dolores and make their way up the vermilion cliffs stained with yellow lichen. Closest to the water are the dull tamarisks, branches drooping in the eddies; here and there among them stand cottonwoods, pale gold warblers flitting in their leaves. Above, clinging to narrow ledges and cracks in the cliffsides, are junipers, their squat forms almost blue in the shadows. To their right and left, perched on improbable aeries and edged in ranks against the sky, grow ponderosa pines – their green so fundamental, serene and cool that every paddle stroke is calmed by their presence.

Through the late afternoon shadows we run one more rapid, eddy into a level clearing surrounded by giant conifers and drag the kayaks and support raft ashore. As we unpack our supplies, the sunlight climbs steadily up the pink buttresses and lights the hanging forest above. The camp stove is lit; tea water is put on; wet suits are hung in the tamarisk to dry. Singly and in couples, the 13 of us find level spots to unroll our sleeping pads, stretch our cramped backs, write an entry in a journal. No one sets up a tent – the sky is too empty for rain. In the dusk we gather around the boiling kettle, open some beers and vegetables for dinner. Stories of other western rivers and Asian mountains are passed back and forth like potlatches. Friends for many years – going back to our instructor days at the Colorado Outward Bound School – we also tell each other about our new jobs: physical therapist, leadership consultant, biologist, Sierra Club representative. Looking at the river, someone says, "A fine day." Our beer cans and tea cups click in salute: to our old friendship, to this lovely river, and to her uncertain future when, dammed and diverted for agriculture and industry, she may flow only several days each year.

Her name, *El Río de Nuestra Señora de Dolores*, The River of Our Lady of Sorrows, came from the explorers of the Spanish province of New Mexico. In 1776, just a few weeks after the Liberty Bell had run out its joyous news in Philadelphia, two holy men, Fathers Francisco Antanasio Domínguez and Silvestre Vélez de Escalante, set out with eight companions and a string of mules and horses from Santa Fe. Following a decade-old commercial route pioneered by the Indian trader Juan María de Rivera, they trekked north, looking for a way to the colony of California. Dropping into the river's steep red rock canyons, they fought their way through its thickets and were at last turned back by the boulder-filled channel. They climbed from the river bed and skirted along the mesatops, at times hungry, thirsty, and ill. When they returned to Santa Fe the following year, having done a giant loop through the future states of Colorado, Utah, Arizona, and New Mexico, they fixed the river's course and her name on their charts. But their adventure, like the Dolores, was soon forgotten.

Perhaps that was to be expected. Their records were deposited in Mexico City and the most celebrated explorer of the region, John Wesley Powell, naturally chose to popularize the greatest feature he visited: the Grand Canyon. Topography also abetted the bypassing of the Dolores. Beginning as a freshet from a melting snowbank on the south side of Lizard Head Pass, not many miles from the town of Telluride, high in the San Juan Mountains of Colorado, the Dolores flows southwest, growing quickly. It passes through the old mining town of Rico, drops into the city limits of Dolores, near where Domínguez and Escalante camped, and makes a hard north bend, turned away from its ancestral course to the San Juan River by an igneous uplift that began about 10 million years ago. In the next 180 miles it cuts through an undulating series of anticlines, the backbone of Colorado's uranium country. Slickrock, Bedrock, Paradox, Uravan – the names of the towns lying near its course are as hard and sun-blasted as the surrounding landscape, a vaguely heart-shaped spread of forested plateau and high desert bounded by Grand Junction in the north, Durango and Cortez in the south, and Moab to the west. Two winding blacktop roads bisect its length and width. Otherwise there's not much in the way of transportation corridors, unless you count the tracks the gold and silver miners put in during the 1800s and the rutted grades the uranium miners scraped out in the 1950s. Driving from Albuquerque to Salt Lake City, or from Phoenix to Denver, you could pass right through the Dolores River country and never know what existed below the sage, the heat mirage, and the tailings.

The rapids start five minutes from camp: Glade, Molar, and Canine. Each has big waves and roaring holes. The air temperature is a pleasant 60°; the water freezes your hand if you trail it by the side of your boat. Pine and loam scents mix in the flying spray; in the pools between rapids, swallowtail butterflies hover over the kayaks. Above, far far above, one golden eagle glides between the canyon walls. Steep side canyons, overgrown with brush and blocked by cliffbands, rise to the east. In that direction the nearest paved road is 40 miles away. Elk and deer scat are on the banks where we stop to collect the group and there's the feel, in the rough and tumble, unkempt look of the country, that black bear call the place home. We're not the only ones of this opinion. In 1973 the Dolores was proposed for inclusion in the study phase of the federal Wild and Scenic Rivers Act. Under President Carter's administration it was recommended. However, Ray Kogovsek, who until 1984 was the congressman in whose district the Dolores lies, was unwilling to introduce such a bill. His successor, Michael Strang, has not taken a position on the issue.

There is a long quiet stretch of slick green water made ominous by increasing thunder. We land river left, walk through the tamarisk and emerge on an outcropping of stone above Snaggletooth Rapid. Named by Otis "Doc" Marston, a World War I submarine commander who first ran the Dolores in 1948, Snaggletooth in high water is a complex series of recirculating holes, powerful hydraulics, and one black monolith of rock, waiting for any boater who doesn't maneuver carefully.

We elect to do a "shoulder run," i.e. – put your kayak on your shoulder and walk safely around. A dirt road comes down to the rapid from the rimrock above and some friendly folks in a pickup help us portage the raft. While we're ferrying equipment several other rafts try the run. Two make it, but a third flips in the first hole. Its two occupants don't appear for nearly a minute. Gasping, they finally surface halfway through the rapid and are swept far downriver before rescuers on shore can help them.

By four-thirty in the afternoon the portage is done, and we run a couple more miles of difficult water before the river flattens and grows glassy. Swallows dive and loop from the cliffs, their chirps mixing with the ever present swish of eddy-suck along the hulls of the kayaks. In a grove of cottonwoods, along a prominent bend of the river, just as the long evening shadows bring relief from the sun, we land and make our second camp.

The day has taken its toll: two cameras wet, one contact lens lost, a cooler flooded. While Kate and Greg cook dinner, Pat, Lucy, and Dave dry tea bags, nuts, and granola on the overturned raft, which also gets a patch job. Sitting in a circle beneath the trees, we eat Kate's tuna and noodles in the last evening light. From downriver comes the faint murmur of more rapids mingling with the cricket pulse. I try to remember in which rapid I rolled and in which I failed and had to swim. I try to pinpoint where it was I saw the canyon wren and where the Wingate sandstone was washed with a stain shiny as ebony. Too tired to think clearly, I run together success and failure, wildlife and geology, until the Dolores flows bend to bend, a timeless merging of sky, cliffs, and juniper, the eddies turning slowly like the Dipper above, our trip joining Marston's and Escalante's and Utes too old to name.

Between the Spanish father on his horse and the submarine commander in his unwieldy duckboat, a different sort of explorer visited the Dolores. In 1885 James W. Hanna helped found the Montezuma Valley Ditch Company, a group intent on building a canal across the low divide separating the Dolores River from the San Juan Basin. The diversion would bring water to the Dolores' ancient, fertile but dry riverbed. By 1907 two canals were in operation and 37,500 acres of the Montezuma Valley were eventually irrigated. The most productive crop was pinto beans. The Dolores, however, became no more than a trickle by early July of each year. Nonetheless, a happy balance was achieved. In the three months of peak spring runoff commercial rafting companies created a trade worth two million dollars annually to the state.

In 1968 the dream of making the desert flower surfaced again. Western water interests pushed the Colorado River Basin Project Act through Congress, its purpose reclamation, irrigation, and water for industry and small agricultural towns. Of the five projects authorized, Animas-La Plata is in the planning stages, and Dallas Creek and Dolores are partially completed. By 1984 McPhee Dam, a 275-foot-high structure below the town of Dolores, was controlling the flow of the river. By 1987 engineers hope to have the reservoir filled to capacity. Then the future becomes murky.

It is certain that there will be an eleven-mile trout fishery below the dam. Also certain are the 1.2 megawatts of power the dam will produce and the recreational benefits of the boat docks, picnic areas, and campgrounds now being built around the reservoir. In addition, it's clear that parts of Dolores and Montezuma counties will receive irrigation water: the pump stations are under construction.

Uncertain is the final cost of the project and thus the price of water at the user's tap. Originally estimated to cost 46 million dollars, the price of the total project has risen to about 420 million, making the cost/benefit ratio marginal to say the least. Dove

Creek, a town of 800 people that bills itself as the pinto bean capital of the world, may have to pay between $4500 and $7000 per capita for its municipal and industrial water.

Nor have farmers had good news. The sprinkler systems that will enable them to use Dolores water for lettuce, hay, and peach production are expensive ($40,000 for a quarter section of irrigated land) and some farmers have chosen not to install them. Ironically, the Dolores River Project—wished for, supported by, and theoretically designed to help the small dry land farmer—may eventually help no one so much as agribusiness firms, which can afford the costs of bringing water to a land better suited to sage and beans.

The unknowns are not only financial. No one can predict whether the elk and deer herds that once migrated across Dolores Canyon to their wintering ground will find substitute terrain around the reservoir. No one in the Bureau of Reclamation is willing to state when and if spills will occur and of what duration and intensity they will be. In fact there may be only ten days of whitewater boating each year.

The Dolores' story is unfortunate and confused, and one which we've heard before on the Tuolumne, the St. Johns, and the Niobrara Rivers. One might ask, why do we not hear about these projects before the dams are in place, the rapids threatened, and the only thing left to do is fight delaying actions, then write eulogies?

The question is more philosophical than factual and perhaps deserves an answer based in emotion, western emotion. Beyond the 100th meridian, a curious mental phenomenon took hold of both explorers and settlers—what might be called an extension of the New World dream, which caused immigrants to believe that on the shores of America anything was possible. They believed they were coming to a paradise instead of what they actually found, a "dismal, howling" wilderness. Beyond the plains of Kansas, under the vast sky rimmed by snowy mountains, this dream took on epic proportions and still holds sway. If the right amount of technological leverage could be exerted, the thinking has gone—just divert the wasted water in some remote canyon to a dry but fertile valley, for instance—and an arid country would turn green.

One of the few Americans to gainsay these fantasies and ground himself in the realities of his environment was none other than John Wesley Powell. In his 1879 *Report On The Lands Of The Arid Region Of The United States,* he made a clear separation between those inaccessible dry lands which were best suited for grazing and those lands to which water could be diverted profitably, allowing crops to be grown. He suggested that the 1862 Homestead Act be amended so that 80 instead of 160 acres become the viable irrigation unit and 2560 acres, or 16 times the alloted husbandman's parcel, be given over to dryland livestock use. No one listened to Powell in the 19th century and few, if any, have listened to him in the 20th.

In the case of the Dolores River Project the deafness has been acute but understandable. Water dreams die hard and a century of wishing that the desert would bloom isn't erased by low cost-benefit ratios associated with expensive dams. In the West dollar signs just aren't equal. Those that create verdure are worth more.

In Mile Long Rapid the fallen sandstone boulders build a labyrinth of white flumes, blue whirlpools, and foaming, squirrelly eddies. Rare on big western rivers, this is the best sort of kayaking: lots of maneuvering, quick decisions, the boats darting from rock to rock. The sky is a soft hazy blue, the canyon broadens as we descend, oak and piñon stretch to its faraway rims. For a moment, there are no roads beyond the line where sky meets earth, no dam behind us, making this perhaps the last full runoff season to be had on the Lady of Sorrows.

Most of the group takes out in Bedrock. Maggie Fox, the Sierra Club regional representative for the Southwest, Greg Grange, an energy consultant in Boulder, and I load our kayaks with some food and our sleeping bags. We push on through Paradox, Mesa, and Gateway Canyons; through Stateline Rapid, big as Snaggletooth; through the Narrows and Beaver Creek drop, where the canyon walls roar with a volume of water swelled by the San Miguel River and tens of side streams caught along the way. Then there are rapids for which we can find no name and hidden draws that seem to have been visited only once or twice since the beginning of time.

On the afternoon of the sixth day the vertical red cliffs fall off to the west and we float through bottomland. In an unremarkable place, just beyond six nesting herons, the Dolores slows to a crawl, gains twice it width, and in a broad gray sheet joins the Colorado. We float a mile down the father of western rivers, which is diverted through every state along its banks and no longer reaches its outlet in the Sea of Cortez. But we don't dwell on that as we eddy our boats to shore, nor on what may happen to the Lady Dolores or her still untouched cousins, the Animas and La Plata. For a moment the confusing interplay of costs and benefits, brought about by trying to live richly in desert country, is forgotten. One stretch of river has been good and we're connected.

Baja

The Spanish, a musical race with a good sense of topographic irony, named the features of the New World with religious fervor and a fanciful turn of mind. They called a whole mountain range Sangre de Cristo, the blood of Christ, and the desolate coast of Baja California after the Amazon queen, Calafia, whose paradise they never found. When it came time to christen the two most alluring bays of that peninsula, they chose the name Concepcion for the one on the Sea of Cortez, and indeed it's a placid anchorage right out of the newmade creation. But for the bay on the Pacific, surrounded by mountains where gales are born, they chose the name of the reformed whore, Magdalena, a woman who, though penitent, never lost the passion of her heart.

Pat and I clung to the gunwales as Manuel, the boatman from Puerto San Carlos, pounded the twenty-foot launch over the whitecaps. Ahead, the brown dry mountains of Isla Magdalena, guarding the bay from the Pacific, began to grow out of the horizon. Behind us the radio tower of San Carlos rose, dipped, and disappeared a final time into the sea. We looked back, trying to memorize a heading for our return paddle, and shared a shrug as we imagined pointing our kayaks into an empty sky.

Within a half hour we found calmer water in the lee of Punta Belcher and ran down the coast of Isla Magdalena another few miles before rounding a final bend. Above us a volcanic headland, Punta Entrada, reared, thrusting like an open hand 300 feet above the Pacific. Directly south by four miles rose another headland, Punta Redondo, and in the strait between these two guardians the ocean rolled.

Manuel cut the engine and we slipped into a cove just a few hundred yards from the point. The water was turquoise for many feet beneath our keel and through a narrow cut in the rocks, no more than ten feet across, we saw the breakers crashing on the Pacific side of the headland. Frigate birds soared in the thermals overhead; curious pelicans skimmed by; with a delicious crunch, the bow scraped the sand.

I started tossing dry bags to Pat while Manuel held the boat. Diving gear, cameras, binoculars, casting rod, tent, sleeping bags, pots, stove, two folding kayaks, ten gallons of water—the pile grew on the beach. As Pat carried up the last duffel, I handed Manuel three one-thousand peso notes. "I can come back and get you in four days," he said. His temptation lasted a moment. "No, it's fine," I told him. "We'll paddle to San Carlos."

He pushed his boat into the sea, leapt aboard, and with a wave and bright smile was gone. Hands in my pockets, I stared at the unruly pile of gear. Pat touched my arm and showed me a shell that she had already ferreted out from the litter of mollusk and snails at our feet: a small luminescent abalone. We looked at her find a moment, then cast a glance at the gear . . . the tent should be pitched, the boats assembled. We looked at each other again . . . we had already spent four days driving from the southern tip of the Baja peninsula just to get to this desolate headland, called by some relieved mariner, "the entrance point." A nod was all the agreement we needed to give each other. She grabbed her binoculars, I my lure pouch, and we dashed through the cut in the headland, eager for the ocean.

On the surfline I cast. The spume pulled at my knees as I threw a spoon into the swell. On the next toss the lure fell into a frothy green whirlpool larger than a house. Kelp streamed into the sea then floated toward me like the hair of a young girl jumping rope, seen in slow motion from above. Stacks of volcanic rock marched northwards along the coast, the breakers smashing on the black walls and filling the air with mist. Keeping time with the breakers I tossed my lure and listened as the sea sang of whale flukes, square riggers, coco palms, and something older. Out of that prehistoric time, five pelicans cleaved the mist – perhaps they were pterodactyls – and lead my eye to where Patricia rounded a headland opposite me and vanished.

Trained as a biologist and toxicologist, Pat Billig is an old friend. In fact, a few nights before, we had tried to remember when we had first met and could hardly recall the year. Like myself, she had worked for the Outward Bound School; but she had also done a stint in East Africa with the Peace Corps and, more recently, had been the director of the Teton Science School in Jackson Hole, Wyoming. Now an environmental consultant, she does freelance work for industry, specializing in how wastes affect wildlife populations. Pat also happens to know the name of most every animal and plant you can point out, as well as how they interrelate, and is one of those rare people who, after a long day's hike, will hear a bird call and run with her binoculars rather than eat the dinner that's waiting.

A tug on my rod took me from my thoughts. After a short run, the fish came in easily. Pushed by the swell, it was left at my feet – a 2½-foot barracuda. I unhooked it and the next wave carried it away. In the tide pool where the fish had lain were black sea urchins and pink anemones. I bent closer for a look, wondering at their sedentary life in the endless wash of the surf; then I had a premonition. Glancing seaward, I spied a large comber bearing down on me. I could hardly move before the wave broke and lifted me off my feet. I grabbed at a stack of rocks and held on as the undertow pulled me away. Another wave was coming on the heels of the first and, as I ran to higher ground, I saw it bury the jetty on which I had been standing.

Now more prudent, I worked my way toward the tip of Punta Entrada, timing my casting with the quiet spaces of the sea. A surf perch followed my lure, rushing angrily and slapping its tail, but he wouldn't strike. Finally giving up on the histrionic fellow, I started chasing the blue and green crabs that scuttled over the rocks, cornering one beneath a loose boulder from which I pried him with the butt of my rod. He looked so helpless as I held him from behind, his claws reaching vainly to bite my hand, that I abandoned the idea of boiling him for dinner and placed him back in his pool, now filled with orange sunlight.

Feeling the day run out on me (and not half of what I wanted to do done!), I hurried back to our camp and dealt with a moment of indecision: should I go diving in the lagoon or put together my boat and paddle around the point to troll deeper water. Pat was nowhere to be seen and I preferred diving with her. So I opted for the boat and soon had the kayak assembled. Stepping my rod into the hole designed for the mast, I trailed a sinking plug out beyond the watchful eyes of the pelicans, sitting like wise old statues on the guano-covered headland.

The double-bladed paddle moved me silently, the rod throbbed, the sun was warm, falling to the west. A half-mile of paddling went by as if I had been doing nothing more exciting than cruising the reservoir near my home in Colorado. Then I rounded the entrance point and was lifted by what seemed to be an endless blue breath. Suddenly I could see the breakers hitting the shore in a white hem, the misty volcanic pillars far up the coast, and the mountains running north and south for miles. Just as suddenly, on a long hissing exhalation, I slid out of sight of the coast and all that that remained were the mountaintops above the swell. I paddled further out on the giddy sea, then made a long turn and trolled close to the point, imagining, as I stayed just outside the waves, my lure swimming by the dropoff. But the pass went unrewarded and I returned to the lagoon.

Pat was setting up the tent. "You looked small out there," she said.

"I felt it."

Together we finished staking down the tent, then Pat lit the stove for dinner. I picked up my rod and lure pouch. She gave me a quizzical glance.

"A few more," I said, "It's the best time."

I found a jetty on which to stand, and from this perch above the waves, sent my spoon out in six directions, fanning the dark water before me. The quarter moon rode a band of bright cloud and lit another jetty to my left. Water surged over this rock-pile and every few casts I sent an extra cast there – to the foaming water where a fish should lie.

Orion, the hunter, appeared, then the Dipper rose, and the sky to the west became a faint gray streak, more memory than light. The line sailed from under my thumb, the spume pulled around my knees. Mist filled the cove and I sent yet another cast to the distant rocks.

This time an answer roiled the swell. The rod bent home against the unknown darkness and the line peeled into the deep as the fish turned broadside to swim with the waves. A white comber appeared where the fish had sounded and slithered toward me. I leapt to shore, giving the fish line. The wave broke where I had been standing and, before I could regain the jetty, two more, equally large, crashed down, soaking me with spray. When I scrambled back to the rocks they were still cascading water into the sea. I reeled; the line was tight. I tried pumping the fish closer. He turned and ran for the entrance to the cove. Again I had to trade places with a threesome of combers, and, when I returned, the fish had lost his strength.

Pumping the rod steadily, I brought him closer, his runs growing shorter and more subdued. Then, on the back of a dark swell, I saw a pink and silver glimmer. I led the fish alongside the jetty and through a canal in the rocks. There I found a ledge that took me down to the water. I went in slowly and lifted the rod. The corvina, for now I could see him, swam around my waist. I reached with the gaff, put it through his lip, and walked out of the surf. He was almost as long as my leg.

Patricia had displayed more confidence than I would have shown. She hadn't cooked the pasta. After I cleaned the corvina, we steamed one of the fillets in butter, lemon and garlic. The other I cut into chunks, laid them in a pot, well-mixed with onions, and covered the whole with lemon juice, making *cebiche*, the marinated fish dish of Central America. It would be our lunch for the next day.

The night wind made it cool enough to wear a jacket and I was glad that we had brought sleeping bags. Throwing mine over me in the tent, I could see the last of the moonlight on the roof; and when I closed my eyes all that remained was Pat's sleepy breathing and the clink of sand.

In the dawn, we needed no more than bathing suits. We paddled beyond the breakers, surfing and playing the boats through a narrow channel in the offshore rocks, and growing accustomed to the swell; we had a lunch of corvina and torts; we dove in the lagoon where orange garibaldi fish hid in the coral.

In the afternoon we walked north along the outer beach, climbing over the volcanic headlands that jutted into the surf and blocked our way. Pat had taken over the rod and soon raised two large red fish, which neither of us could identify. As she changed lures, a sea lion emerged from the deeper water with a grouper in its mouth, the tail of the fish lashing wildly. The seal smiled at us, as if giving testimony to its angling skill, before diving out of sight.

At last we came to a promontory around which we couldn't walk or climb. Mirroring our dismay, a front of clouds moved from the north, the sun disappeared and the waves turned a dull lead color. But we could see that the front would soon pass. Pat gave me back the rod, took her camera pack, and returned to camp, saying that she wanted to climb to the top of Punta Entrada again, to watch the sun set. Wanting another fish more than the view, I worked my way back slowly, casting to the likely sloughs and raising nothing. Before an hour had gone by, the sun emerged from the clouds and rain began to fall in great shining yellow draperies. In seconds my cotton pants were soaked through, but the rain felt cool against my skin and sweet after all the salt bathing. I looked away from the setting sun, to the south, and sure enough it appeared—a rainbow over Punta Entrada, arcing from Magdalena Bay to the Pacific Ocean. Pat would be taking good photos. Not having my camera, I made a shot-in-mind: casting harder, I let the wind carry the lure far over the waves and, lifting my arms, I tried to fly out with the line, into the sky, the mist, and the foaming surf. Considering how much magic was pouring from the sea, it was no surprise that I met kindred spirits: from the north, leaping the whitecaps, more than a hundred sea lions raced through the cove.

The sun lit them for a moment before it fell into the western sea, and the surf became dark blue limed with pink, as the light slid out of the sky and the moon took over the heaven. Across its crescent three ghostly pelicans slipped, their necks tucked in, their wings spread to glide. And I wondered, as I watched them soar beyond the last dark pillar, of those other ghost travellers, the sea lions, and if they had put the fish down, tainting my persistence with ill fortune this final evening at the point. I thought about it only once as I cast into the dark. It seemed such a small thought. When I couldn't see anymore, hearing only occasionally the lure slap the water, I returned to the beach, guided by the glow of something white and faintly recognizable. In a few more steps I saw Patricia's bare legs. Seated on the rocks, she had been watching.

The wind gave us little time for farewells. It beat strong out of the north so even our lagoon was filled with small whitecaps. Beyond, in Magdalena Bay, the sea ran deep blue and strong, laced with white. We packed in an hour, not lingering, and pointed the kayaks into the surf where a big wave floated us free. There was hardly time to look back – the cut where we had camped, the proud tall headland, the frigate birds still circling above it. We had to paddle straight into the whitecaps, which occasionally broke over the boats and foamed around our waists, snug and dry in their spray skirts. It was hard steady work, but the kayaks rose easily on the waves and slid cleanly into the next trough.

We paddled for two days into the wind, edging our way north along the coast of Isla Magdalena and finally leaving its shore for the far horizon. We quartered across the wind for a couple hours, and just as the mirage-line to the east began to shape itself into coco palms and shacks, the headland fell into the waves – like old friends meeting, or a paddle well done, no more than a temporary signature between a retreating and an appearing horizon.

Cash Flows

Walking down the street the other day, I was feeling sorry for myself. Like the pronoun in the previous sentence, my problems were center stage. And with good reason. I was out of money. Such a sad state can happen to anyone, let alone a writer, whose income is subject to editorial whims, draughts of cash flow at the magazines to whom he sells, and his own rising and falling creative energies. Having been broke before, I had decided to protect myself from these economic pitfalls by writing for many markets, by choosing magazines that seemed to have money in their coffers, and by treating writing like any other job: at my desk Monday through Friday (most weeks) and while on assignments, moonlighting, that is I'd gather information for a couple speculative stories in addition to the one I knew I would sell.

But chance is playful and recently, when I returned from a long trip in the North, I found that a series of coincidences had accumulated, producing a zero in my check book. First and foremost, an article on physical fitness that I had done for *Sports Afield* had been thought too long and needed pruning. It lay on my desk, unpaid for. Their art director had also been on vacation and had neglected to put through a payment requisition for a fly-fishing photo I had shot months before. To make matters worse, *Cross-Country Skier's* cash flow was off due to a lack of advertising in the summer months. So yet another $1500 sat in limbo, and, having been a nice guy, I had agreed to receive payment for a long feature upon its publication – months away. The disaster continued. *Audubon*, though having bought a text of mine in the spring, still hadn't decided about the accompanying photos, and *Outside's* sad story, related to me on the phone, was that their accountant, without whom the issuing of payments could not be accomplished, had had triple bypass surgery and had just returned to work. "Your check is in the mail," they assured me.

That's what I decided to tell the bank which holds my mortgage, but I thought it wouldn't go over too well. So, feeling left in the lurch by my magazines, I walked downtown, muttering curses and threats, feeling abject and abandoned, and wondering for the umpteenth time if we penpushers shouldn't unionize. Eventually I reached the Trident Cafe where I write, chat, berate the government, tell tall tales, and console and receive consolation from friends. Standing in front of the screen door, out of which came the aroma of coffee and croissants, I calculated if I could afford a capuchino to assuage my frustrations.

At that very moment a tall, skinny, long-haired and bearded man, a leftover flower child of the sixties, walked by, peered into the door and said, "Hi." A cigarette drooped in the corner of his mouth and I knew he was going to ask me for a dime.

Instantly, I knew I was mistaken. You can't even buy a phone call for a dime anymore.

"Say," he said, "could you spare fifty cents?"

I am the softest touch. Besides, I knew I wasn't *really* out of money. After all, by simply making the 8 of the bank's zip code into a 5, I could have my mortgage check sent to St. Paul, Minnesota instead of Denver, Colorado, and in the ensuing delay and the time it took for the bank to cash my check (with no penalty since the envelope's postmark would prove when I had mailed it), I could write another check for a hundred bucks that would carry me through groceries, capuchinos, and the *Sunday Times* until some magazine, staving off its creditors with equally devious machinations, paid me. Isn't this the way America rolls on?

The fellow in the doorway of the cafe didn't seem to have recourse to such ploys. So I fished out four bits and feeling smug dropped the quarters in his outstretched palm.

He looked at the coins as if they might not be real. The smell of coffee was nearly overwhelming. Having another quarter ready, I said, "Coffee's sixty cents."

He closed his fist and took a happy step toward the corner where a flower vendor sat. Over his shoulder, he said "I'm going to buy a carnation for a lady."

Breaking Three

In the dark hours of the morn, the buses rumble toward the desert. After a twenty-five mile drive, let off at the junction of two sandy roads, we begin to walk through the saguaro cactus towards the mountains. There are several hundred of us, and now and then someone in the group stops and stares up at the stars, as if taking a bearing in case we get lost. Shortly, we see the glow of electric lights and the mutter of a loudspeaker. A middle-aged woman in front of me turns around, looks back toward Phoenix, and sighs.

But the dawn has gathered in the east, a faint pink smudge lying over the desert, and in another minute our feet strike tarmac. We walk under a banner that declares the annual running of the Fiesta Bowl Marathon, sponsored by the Scottsdale Charros, a Phoenix running club. It's doubtful that anyone has gotten on the bus by mistake, yet by the expressions on some people's faces—anguish, fear, resigned doom—one would think that they had made a serious error back at the hotel. A few of these folks bolt to the bushes to relieve the call of their nervous intestines.

I pick up my bib and after safety-pinning it to my singlet I stand in the starting line, shaking out my hands and watching those around me shake out theirs. Some runners, lean and skitterish as greyhounds, rapidly touch their toes, while others, content as waddling geese, breathe deeply and meditatively, their eyes closed. I glance around, looking for someone who might be a better pacer than these two extremes of runnerdom, someone who, like myself, is not in this part of the lineup to win the race or gratify his ego by starting toward the front, but who wishes to do no more – or less – than break the three-hour barrier. No one really fits the bill.

To my left are three knobby-kneed ten-year-olds, jumping up and down and contorting themselves into yogi-like stretches. Directly behind them is a tall parched man, close to seventy. He rolls his head in a slow circle while letting his arms hang loosely at his sides. His ribs show in his chest, and he has such little flesh upon his extremities that it appears that he might vanish, like a dry seed pod, in the next strong wind. I think that I'll be faster than he, but then looks can be deceiving. I've run races in which similar gents have sailed by me never to be seen again.

I search some more, turning around to spot – and simultaneously smell – two lime-fresh, tan, and chatty women all in white. Country club foxes for sure, with legs that would make girls much their juniors envious. They're not pacers but the view from the rear would be nice. They give me big smiles, which I return, and then I crane my neck and look over their heads in one last effort to spot someone who has jogged through a couple marathons and is now ready to race one. But the faces dissolve – here a blue stone earring, there a swarthy Navajo grin – as the field of nearly 5000 stretches into the distance and becomes a blur.

My attention is drawn back to the banner where the quiet has grown perceptible. Seven-thirty is obviously near, for everyone has edged forward, is standing on tiptoe, is leaning expectantly toward the open road, lying straight, clean and beckoning like a promise of freedom. Everyone, no matter what their conditioning or background, would like to run the coming 26 miles 385 yards well. For some that will mean simply finishing. For a few it will mean battling for first place. For me it means running at least one second under the magical, elusive, and wonderfully pointless three hour mark. The gun barks; ten thousand feet slowly begin to move; someone cheers.

As the pack shifts, accelerates and lags, two men appear from nowhere and fall into stride by my shoulder. They are from Denver, one dark, one blond, and we go along happily together, talking about training methods and the cool weather. They seem like just the sort of fellows I need: serious about what they do, breezy about how they do it. The darker man has run five marathons in the last ten months – a perfect pacer. But at mile 3, as I begin to hurry and they slow, I have a premonition that we won't see the finish together. "What time are you shooting for?" I ask.

"Three-twenty," the fairer says and the darker one adds, "I'm tired."

So, reluctantly, I pull away. The number of runners bunched across the road makes it difficult to keep a steady pace and after weaving for a hundred yards I drift onto the sandy shoulder and cruise alone. The pack becomes a moving streak of blue and red to my right – they in one energy flow, I in another. Within a few seconds I forget them and begin to study my shadow rippling on the sand and the easy spill of my breath. Face parting the wind, I float up the hills.

As I go through the five-mile aid station and grab a cup of E.R.G., the flat-tasting electrolyte fluid doled out at these races, I hear my time shouted from the sidelines. It's still too slow and I accelerate up the road, thinking of strategies.

There are two ways to run a given time in the marathon. In the first method you calculate the average time per mile you must maintain throughout the race. For three hours this turns out to be 6 minutes and 52 seconds per mile. Keeping such a pace for every one of the 26 miles is rarely successful unless you have the spirit of an automaton. Most flesh and blood runners, in whose middle ranks I include myself, use the slow-beginning/fast-finish method, the logic of which is to get ten miles done at a 6:55–7:00 pace. You then race the last fifteen miles for all you're worth, trying to achieve a 6:20–6:30 pace. Even after taking into account your inevitable slowdown during the last few miles, the two paces average out to around 6:52 and you break three hours – or so you dream from the comfort of your den with your calculator, notepad, and glass of lemonade before you.

Far more than being physically the more practical method of running a marathon, the slow-beginning/fast-finish strategy has significant psychological advantages over the steady state theory. You arrive at mile 10 actually fresher than when you began the race, your muscles having become supple through exercise. You can then begin with an uplifed heart to pass those in the field who were caught in the most jejune of strategies – the jackrabbit start – and have expended themselves disastrously in the excitement and joie de vivre of the first hour.

Any schoolchild can see, though, that ten miles plus fifteen miles equals only twenty-five miles, leaving one and one-quarter miles left to run. This is not an error. The last 2145 yards are simply not figured into the equation. They are the part of the marathon for which no equation is possible. They are run on will and on desire, and occasionally on some deeper faith that you find within yourself.

At the ten mile aid station, hearing the time I want, I fling the empty cup of E.R.G. aside with glee (where else except the marathon can we litter with such a clean conscience?) and skim up the road, passing those who were ahead of me on the last hill. The road has been closed to traffic, the air is still and cool, everything seems right for breaking three hours: my legs are light and free, my arms strong and flexible. Imagining myself a bird, a swooping blue and gray swallow, I fly on.

Miles 12, 13, and 14 are a windsong. My heart beats peacefully, sweetly, as if I were taking a stroll. I actually make humming noises going down the hills, like a diving airplane; my feet hardly touch the ground.

As I come into the 15-mile aid station I hear another time and congratulate myself on my months of training – all those sixty-mile weeks that have left me fit. If this were the end of the race I could trot home feeling self-satisfied, sleek, well-groomed and put away a breakfast of pancakes within a half hour of showering.

Instead I gulp my E.R.G. and push up the road with a sudden hint of nausea following my traditional belch. I file this first sign of weariness into my subconscious and weave quickly through the pack. At mile 16, going up a hill, I try to catch three men, all in pinstripe singlets. They are running a good race as well and it takes a tangible effort to overtake them and keep the pace over the crest. There's no denying it – the Centaur is gone from my thighs. On the long flats ahead I begin to concentrate on my hand position and the angle of my lower back, those fine touches to which I gave no thought a few miles ago.

A time is shouted at the 17-mile mark. I'm doing better than I expected. I shall be several minutes under three hours at this rate. For an instant I slow, gratified, then I correct and speed up, knowing what is bound to come.

At 17½ miles – after having now pushed quite a few miles down into the low 6-minute range – the bill collector knocks. I am struck by a sudden wilting sensation when I stop to drink. It's not weariness, rather a disinclination to be doing this any longer. How nice it would be to sit by the shoulder of the road and watch the clouds evaporate over the mountains, to sing a song, to count the needles of a saguaro cactus, and fall asleep under a juniper. The first 150 yards from the aid station passes in reverie before I slap my mind hard and bring myself back to the road.

At 19 miles the pain starts in earnest. A gripping cramp, a cringing spasm, a stabbing under my ribs. Going faster and breathing more quickly only increases this catastrophe inside my thoracic cavity. Of course I can slow down. And of course that will ruin my chances of breaking three hours. But slowing down is only one of three options. Without breaking stride, I explore the other two. I can maintain this pace and bear the pain, which is exactly what I'm doing. Or I can increase the pace and, by instituting an alternate form of torture, perhaps forget the spear turning under my ribs. I choose the latter option and cut ten seconds off the next mile.

The course turns into the wind. Traffic now moves on the opposite side of the road, and the sun has come out from behind the morning haze. I can feel the salt drying on my forehead, my lips stretched taut, my tongue big in the roof of my mouth. Two creatures are now running this race, and one can feel the other's pain and emotions. Then the voices begin: "Who are you doing this for? Don't hurt yourself. There's always another race."

"I've trained for months." This voice is angry. "I've watched my diet. I ran in the dark, in the snow. There is no other race. This is it."

"You should have run more intervals," the other says.

"It was icy. I didn't have the time."

"You didn't want to make the time. Intervals, fartlek, 440s at the track. You wouldn't be hurting so much now."

"Next time."

"You said this was it."

"I know."

I try to go faster but the iron maiden clamped to my side has sapped my will. I go into and out of the 20-mile aid station feeling as if my legs are made of glue. I want to speed up yet I can't think of any reason why I should. To stop, to rest, just for ten seconds is all I want. But if I stop only once, I know I shan't begin again. Oh, where is the joy of the first miles? Why did I ever want to break three hours?

This self-pity lasts perhaps 50 yards before I replace it with a more satisfying emotion – anger. I curse at the merciless side-stitch. I order it to leave me alone. I actually punch my ribs twice. But the sidestitch, like a terminal illness, remains, and I have to search for another reason to go on. It's no longer a question of breaking three hours. I want simply to run my best, to not give in to this demon that's crippling me, that wants to humble me to the shoulder of the road, to make me into a figure of defeat – drooped head, downcast shoulders, walking in while the others run through their penance.

As I look at those already limping by the side of the road, I think of my wife meeting me at the airport and her simple question, "How did you do?" The answer, "I hurt so much at 20 miles I had to stop," sounds too pathetic to contemplate. Better to die out here. I look around. It wouldn't be a bad place to die, under the blue sky, in a valley fringed by mountains on a cool December day.

A runner shouts a time. I couldn't have heard him right. I ask him again and he shouts, "Two twenty-two." My heart leaps. Yes, yes, I can still break three hours. And oh, God, that's really all I want – just to go from one meaningless point on the earth to the next, this arbitrary distance chanced upon by poor Pheidippides and lengthened by British whimsy, this point A to point B in 180 minutes and not a second more. Then I'll die happy.

So bear the pain. Endure it. It's not that bad. It's not as bad as in

Denver, not nearly as bad. There you almost walked. And here in Phoenix you're still passing people. But why can't you ever find someone to run with? Someone to keep beautiful 6:20s and carry you in their draft across the finish line. Where is the perfect pacer?

There. I hurry over to a thin man in red shorts and run in his shadow. Shielded by his body, I go faster for a moment; but it's only an illusion. He's running slightly slower than I am and I have to pass him. As I pull out from behind him, the wind hits me in the chest. I increase my stride to compensate and shooting pains go down my hamstrings. I break stride for a few steps, realizing that my body is entering a state of total collapse, a complete shutdown. I see a tree and a shady spot of grass beneath it. Suddenly I want to stop. Nothing else matters. Nothing. I streak by the tree, feeling a blush of shame. What would my friends think? I know that most of them won't even bother to ask me about the race, that by the time I see some of them weeks will have passed and the marathon will be forgotten. But what if, six months down the road, one of them asks, 'How did you do in Phoenix?" I would like to say, "I did well." Wanting to say that, I push the next hill.

In this way – accusation, counter-accusation, self-recrimination – two miles go by like a week in which I've had much on my mind, and, going to hang up some clothes that I threw on a chair on Tuesday, I realize with a start that it's Sunday night. I pass the 22-mile sign.

Wind blows at my legs; the road glares; all around is barren desert. I overtake people with spittle drooling down their chins, their arms slack, their eyes glazed, each suffering through his private bouts of shame, his snatches of heroism. In the distance, like an Old Testament vision, glint the buildings of Phoenix and the end.

I drink at 22½; touch my toes. Don't linger! Out I go, hard as I can muster. Three more runners fall behind me. I pass them without emotion and watch the clouds in the distance, throwing my mind up into their softness and peace.

They remind me of great mountains, of the Ivanhoes of my youth and strength. Adventure, determination, courage – I want to hear those words now. Where are the Little Johns with whom I shared so much, with whom I was bold and risked all?

But I don't hear their voices nor can I see their grins. There are no trumpets, only quiet. And in that strange silence, through which I hear my feet pounding, in this landscape where the heat waves shimmer across the near and the far, I suddenly think of my parents far away, spending an ordinary day as their bit of recreated protoplasm runs across a desert they have never seen nor would care to see.

There is my father commuting to the same job on the same train, buying the same paper and the same cup of coffee as he has each day for the last thirty years. There he is still moving quickly through the morning crowds with a smile of satisfaction, work making his heart light, a man of whom Tennyson might have written, "That ever with a frolic welcome took/The thunder and the sunshine." And there was thunder enough, especially when his offspring became wayward and his wife, a small, unathletic, but very religious woman, nearly broke down when confronted by children she couldn't understand, much less respect. She condemned for a long time, then, at the last possible instant, took her Kierkegaardian leap toward us all, leaving behind some cherished proprieties. That leap hurt her with a pain none of us could imagine, a sort of guilt and despair that few of us, raised in this easy come-easy go time, have experienced. Yet she bore up and said, when she had at last seen us all survive and prosper, that it was prayer and faith that had seen her through. We were having a breakfast cup of coffee, just she and I, and I wanted a more empirical answer than faith and prayer to hang my hat upon. Knowing her son, she said, "Oh, I decided that pain, like grace, was only temporary."

Godspeed, Mam.

Mile 24 goes under but I can see the last aid station in the distance. I look beyond it, toward the red hot air balloon that floats above the finish. I look back to the road and see the aid station closer. The balloon . . . the clouds . . . the calm blue sky . . . under my ribs the jackhammer pain. The aid station coming fast. I hear the time, do a quick calculation, and blast through without stopping. I need a five-minute mile. I begin to sprint.

A short man with a beard tries to catch me. I speed up, he fades. He tries to catch me again. Again I shake him. A half mile goes by, his breath on my shoulder. My breath whips in and out, and deep under my breath I can hear a moan that comes from someone who is not myself, a supplication that is weary beyond belief, that comes from someone who no longer has anything to give.

In two and a half minutes you can rest. In two minutes you can rest. In a minute and a half you can rest.

At the last turn the bearded man pulls by my shoulder, takes a step past me, his face grimacing, his mouth wrenched open. No. I turn it on and lose him.

The times are being called a quarter mile away. A blur of cheering spectators lines the chute; the hot air balloon floats above them. I try to catch the runner before me. I have to catch him. He is trying to catch the man in front of him. If I catch them both in these last 200 yards, I know I'll have run well. I kick and am shocked to find nothing, absolutely nothing, not even a moan. My legs are putty, I feel myself going under, push on.

Two men, gasping, crying, slavering from nowhere, rush pell-mell from behind me and beat me by a yard to the finish line. They are 450th and 451st. I am 452nd.

An aid puts his arm around my waist and, as he leads me down the chute, I hear the loudspeaker say that I missed three hours by two minutes and a little more.

Market Day

A good day in the Big Apple. Third to Park to 55th. Editors and I look at slides of the Arctic Ocean, of caribou, and musk ox while faint noises of traffic circulate far below. There is a now-famous *New Yorker* cartoon that shows the Manhattanites' view of North America. Midtown Manhattan, the Hudson, and New Jersey occupy half the cartoon. The Great Plains, the Rockies, the southwestern deserts, the Golden Gate, the Pacific, and China occupy the other half, compressed as if viewed through a long telephoto lens. Today nearly the same compression occurs as a continent and a good part of its wildlife are admired and chosen for publication – all from a few rooms in tall buildings.

Bending over a light table, I peer at animal friends through the 8x magnification of a lupe, just as I peered at them a few short weeks ago through a camera lens while they forded cold rivers and stood on rocky pinnacles above glaciers. Five thousand miles to the northwest, they are no doubt doing much the same, chewing their cuds, scratching, suckling, as New York begins to flicker under tungsten.

We talk, my editor friends and me, about this project and future ones, and afterwards as I stroll down Fifth Avenue – like a pilot or sea captain happiest cast-off – I try to visualize East Africa and how within a few months I'll return to these towers with more slides, more captured spirit to be mailed to readers who will peer at it while on the john or after dinner, perhaps even in shacks not far from where the spirit was originally stalked.

It's an odd circle, we oxpeckers on the back of some vast dark ungulate who moves beneath us, who feeds us, but of whose true shape and beginnings we are only marginally aware – through the window of photographs, the imaginative spume of words, through our own small wanderings in the backcountry, if we take the time.

And of we emissaries – traveling between New York and the outbacks, feeding our wanderlust by recording fragmentary portraits of the beast – what might be said of us some day? That we brought the beast's blush to the cities, which lived upon its bloom; that we reminded ourselves of the value of silence; that we kept some continence in an age that didn't have enough? Perhaps . . . and also this: that we returned a gift to the territories, giving them their continued existence by helping to nudge certain souls towards appropriate actions – making phone calls, writing checks, pulling ballot machine handles – all of which left an oil field undeveloped here, an airport unstarted there, the beast allowed to be, to procreate by those who admired it and were willing to pay for its image. Once hunters, we've all become farmers, no one more than I, making this twice-annual trip to market, to sell the stock, trade in and buy new tools, learn what slice of the beast's rump will be in demand next season.

My feet this spring afternoon – caribou calving on the North Slope, ladies in pink leotards eating pretzels on the steps of St. Patty's – lead me to the library whose doors are guarded by lions (lions dozing on the Serengeti tonight and hippos laughing there too, I bet). I have some time before my plane leaves and use it to wander through an exhibition called, "English Illustrated Books of the 19th Century." Near the end of the exhibition is a lovely old folio by Edward Young, which is entitled *Night Thoughts*. The watercolor accompanying the second night is by William Blake and shows a young angel flying into a sky so blue and innocent that, in the marble silence of the New York Public Library, I hear the song of stellar whales. But Blake was never one to leave the babe unblemished. To the right ankle of this celestial diplomat is attached a black chain against which the angel tugs and which, at its other end, disappears into a close of thorns.

The watercolor is worth a few minutes study—more. And when I finally walk into the traffic, toward the shuttle and JFK, I tuck the angel into my mental rucksack and leave his irons. It's not a good idea, when you're hunting the beast, to carry extra baggage or make too much noise.

Neva Hurry

"Billy Joe," I said, "what make you live so long?"

The old Carib fisherman squatted by his palm bark fire, shifting coals with a piece of coconut shell. He wore shorts made out of a flour sack. Behind him, on the far side of the lagoon, the blue Honduras waves broke.

"Such questions," he said, shaking his head.

I waited while he stared at the fire and a slow brown smile crossed his face. He glanced at me. "Mista Ted," he said, "you mus neva, neva hurry. Sun she come up, sun she go down. But man mus neva hurry." Billy Joe, fingers scarred from handlines, gave a nod.

Memories, like dormant seed kernels, pop open from the pressure of the schedule. My appointment book says: FLY N.Y., FLY VEGAS, FLY ANCHORAGE. The phone begins to ring at 7:00 AM, which is 9:00 AM on the East Coast. While I talk I watch the Elk Mountains outside my window, snow-covered from the Colorado winter, begin their cycle of spring avalanches. In time to the ringing of the phone, the slides come down the mountainsides. On one windswept ridge a crescent of bare rock is left. It grins at me, still on the phone, like the slow smile of old Billy Joe, saying "neva hurry."

His words are now a dozen years in the past, as are our good times: eating red snapper on the Belice coast, baking Johnny Cake in a sawed-off oil drum, sailing his 14-foot, rag-rigged sloop. Going nowhere.

Same time of year now – April. But when I look out the windows the only sign of spring is twenty miles downvalley where the new-dropped calves wag their tails and the earth smells wet and fertile. Here at 9,000 feet we still have three feet of snow on the ground, and the cold afternoon sleet showers make sitting indoors, at the desk, not that hard.

At 6:00 PM I make my last calls. It's 5:00 PM on the West Coast, only 3:00 PM in Fairbanks, AK. At 7:00 I finally hang up. Mountain Standard Time is the ideal home for a writer. It lets him work across the continent in twelve-hour days.

As I finish my notes I seem to hear a noise, a low murmur, an undercurrent vibrating the desk. I've been fairly tired, rundown even, so I rub my eyes and pop my jaws, hoping I'm not playing host to flu. No use. The hum remains. I try walking outside, onto the dirt road . . . and listen. The hum seems to come from down the road, and I follow it to the bridge where I put my foot on the railing and look at the creek below. Snowbound for the past four months, the channel is now eight feet wide and running cold and blue. As I watch, a piece of the snowbank drops into the water like a man waking from a dream.

Small bubbles, the color of a muskrat, follow the snow downstream, and I trace their course into the shadow under the bridge. The shadow is deep, cool, and private and lets me imagine the creek flowing on to the Slate River, a mile below town. A few miles further on, the Slate joins the East and powerful, filled with melt, the two rivers flow as one, past the new calves tasting their first grass and the kingfishers, perched on fence posts, watching the riffles at the junction of the East and the big Taylor. No snow there, not a bit. Like a kingfisher on my bridge perch, I picture the dark snakey forms of trout, waking to the spring, their pools filling with the first fallen feed from the uncovered banks.

Thinking of trout, I walk back to the house whose roof, eaves, and yard lie covered by one great drift of snow, whose windows gleam like the eyes of some old prospector crazed with cabin fever. At my desk again, I glance at the appointment calendar. The upcoming days are tightly scheduled and as precisely planned as a space mission's countdown. How did you get yourself so locked in? I wonder, and, suddenly, a good angel, my Carib friend's words echo in the murmur of the creek, in the spume-soft whoosh of long-gone waves, "Neva hurry, man."

Unfortunately it's already dark, too late to go fishing tonight. Besides there isn't a single fly rod in the house. An oversight? Hardly. Colorado's Elk Mountains, from December to April, have need of fly rods the way Key West needs down parkas. My rods, my waders, creel and fly box – *todo, todo, todo*, as the Spanish would say – are 250 miles away in the Boulder house, waiting until next week: see, it's right there on the appointment calendar – "Pick up fishing gear."

Lot of good that does me today when the winter's hurry has come to a head; when the prospect of hurrying through the upcoming weeks until I leave for Alaska becomes unbearable; when all I want to do is hurry to the East River – to wade, to cast, to listen . . . to hurry to where I can slow down. And I have no tackle.

Bemused, looking like an old mountain goat who has gotten himself onto a narrow ledge from which both return and advance appear equally dubious, I sit at my cluttered desk, surrounded by my maps of the exotic places of the world. There should be no complaints. I've been to South America, Asia, and Alaska in the space of three years. I've caught rainbows, goldens, cutthroats, browns, grayling, and the magnificent arctic char. In a few short weeks I'll be back where the char run silver from the Bering Sea. Yet all I wish for on this April dusk is to stand, like years ago, in a small river near home – having been through no airport, having taken no exciting bush flight – while I listen to the sound of hometown fish, swirling their tails against some minor current.

Sun, she went down. Sun she came up. I worked the morning and then plugged the phone into the tape machine. Rummaging here and there, I found the little pack rod that had gone to Alaska the summer before. Throwing a pile jacket and wind pants in the car, I drove to Gunnison. There, in the True-Value hardware store, I bought some crack Korean hip waders. I didn't need any flies. Along with the pack rod was a small plastic tube which contained what I needed: a hare's ear nymph.

The car coasted onto the grass by the banks of the East as the sun sat on the western hills. Even here, twenty miles downvalley from home, snow still lined the river's edge. Nonetheless, the East was open and splashing among its rocks.

I put the split shot two feet up from the nymph and, as I walked to the river, I saw in the same instant a little brown stone fly by my foot and an unidentified insect rush away over the riffles. "Bueno," I said and ambled in.

The water surged green, filled with tawny streamers and white pennants, a parade let loose to greet me. I stopped at my knees, leaning naturally against the current, the air heady with wet grass, cottonwood bark, cold stone smell. Up valley the snow-covered peaks stood frozen and dormant, their summer still three months away. Then from behind the cottonwoods a cow lowed and another answered.

On the second cast there came a tiny bump and the tip of my pole nodded like the head of a divining rod. Not quick enough. I smiled. Working the eddy behind a foaming boulder again and again, I found nothing else and moved on. Unconsciously, letting my feet meander, I explored the fundament of the river with deep slow joy, the way I remember touching a lover who, gone for months, had returned to me. The thought proved too over-powering. I slipped and caught myself with an extended hand. Now wet to the elbow, I continued to walk, surprised that the cold pressure of the jacket on my arm felt wonderful.

The pool emerged after a dip in the river. It was a dark pool, dark as the bridge shadow over which I had stood the evening before, dark as the slow brown smile of Carib Billy Joe and as smooth, glossy, and continually moving as one's life in retro-spect – when all the mindless hurry, inscrutable hurt, and senseless ambition have passed into what we kindly call wisdom. Into this pool, with a delicate plop, I dropped my hare's ear nymph.

It rode halfway down and then this nymph – this divinity of the summer forest, trees and mountains, this bride, this muse, this helpmate – stopped. From past experience and by the evidence before me – a throbbing rod – I became convinced that a trout was on the line. This empiricism hardly indicates the instinctual, psychological, purely emotional response that occurred. I gave a tremendous whoop, which stampeded the contentedly grazing cows, and of course I also immediately fell into the river, shipping water over my starboard hip wader.

"Man, neva hurry."

Yes, Billy Joe, yes.

Rod high, I let the fish zip up and down the pool. When she was tired I led her through a miniature Gibraltar of stones, coasted her across some riffles, and with a gentle thumb and forefinger, so as not to startle her, lifted her from the East. She stretched 14½ inches and, by the laws of this section of the river, went back to breed.

I had to hold her a long time in the current as she worked her jaws and gills. Finally she flapped her tail and slipped from my open palms the way a canoe filled with friends slips away, the way, hand on the rear bumper of your car, you wave goodbye to a child going off to college. I left my hands in the water, exactly where the trout had been, and let them grow cold.

Another old fishing buddy of mine – old in both the chronological sense and in the sense of time gone by – used to rinse his mouth with salt water each time we went on the sea. He said it kept him healthy and he was not reluctant to swallow the mouthful, claiming that it made him both strong and thankful, as well as enabling him to concentrate more deeply on the habits of striped bass, the secretive migrations of mullet, and the evanescent drift of currents, hidden carefully from any man who, as he said, let salt water touch only his skin.

The sun, she had now gone down, and two mergansers, their white bodies glowing in the fading light, flashed upriver. The beat of their wings stayed in my ears long after they had vanished. Then the cows lowed again, convinced that the maniacal whoop they had heard had been nothing more than an aberration of their bovine brains. Though the fish I had caught had long since vanished, I left my hands in the river, in the spot from which I'd released her, listening to mergansers and cows and the swirl of hometown trout, until my fingers were beautifully numb to the bone.

A Trophy Line

Every sport has its trophies. In fishing it might be taking a world record on light tackle. In motor car racing it could be winning a Grand Prix. In back country skiing it's the line.

Exactly what constitutes a line isn't difficult to explain. Even the track skier can see its attributes if pointed in the right direction. Seen from afar, it's the route a ball would take if dropped from a mountain summit, a direct, sweet plummet to the valley floor, sometimes referred to as the fall line. In winter this descent will offer the ski mountaineer, who has climbed a nearby ridge so as not to mar his canvas, an untracked expanse of snow on which to inscribe his signature – a snaky series of linked S turns.

That's one sort of line, the heart and soul of the alpine day tour. As in all forms of trophy acquisition – duck hunting, marathon racing, queuing up for Rolling Stones tickets – these day tours begin in the dark. Wondering why you've left hearth and home, contemplating your frosty breath against the stars, you bushwack to treeline and, too hot, too cold, never just right, climb towards outer space – more astronaut than skier. At the top you take off your traction-skins and put on more clothing. Then you dig a snowpit to check avalanche conditions. If all seems well, you remove your safety straps (in case your stability evaluation isn't spot on), recheck your avalanche transceiver and, taking a deep breath (you never know which one might be your last), swoop down the face. At the bottom . . . Bingo! You've bagged a day tour line.

Not more elegant, but quite a bit more sustained, more replete, and perhaps more satisfying is the high line. A multi-day excursion, such a line connects valleys, high passes, long ridges, steep descents, and an occasional day tour line thrown in to add spice to the bag. Of course you must carry on your back, in addition to all the clothes you need, a tent, a stove, cooking gear, and food to last the trip. This naturally makes the skiing more difficult (ever try to ski with 50 or 60 pounds on your back?). Hence any day tour lines that you pick up along the way, as well as the descents from the passes – if you ski them well – prove more valuable.

But as in any sport there are lines and there are Lines. A true trophy line does not stick its head up around every corner. No sir.

It must be searched out, stalked, tracked, and followed to its lair. Usually, in fact always, this is done with the assistance of topographic maps and beer. A few line hunters will gather around the living room floor, open a six pack, pour a bag of pretzels into a bowl, and connect all the quadrangles in the county and the next, especially if they're hunting for a particularly old and well-endowed line.

In essence what they're looking for is no different from what an Alaskan guide looks for when sizing up a head through his spotting scope: height, breadth, symmetry, and that indefinable but immediately apparent "something" called character.

A trophy line climbs over 12,000 foot passes, it traverses even higher ridges, it has handsome proportions. Below and to each side precipitous valleys fall into dark forests. Toward the horizon other magical ranges recede until they, too, disappear into the sky. As a final test such a line must connect a romantic starting point to an enchanted terminus by an adventurous passage. Even the names of the stopping points along the way ring with arctic tones, chivalrous deeds, strength and courage: Frigid Air Pass,

Paradise Divide, Snowmass Mountain. Lest you think I made up such names, look on any map of Colorado. Those names connect a trophy line.

As with all true trophy seeking, I failed to attain my objective not once, not twice, not even did I score on the third, fourth, fifth, and sixth attempts. You see, such lines are elusive.

Foremost there is the weather. Inevitably it's bad. Now bad weather at 5000 feet is child's play. At 11,000 feet bad weather is not quite child's play, but it's definitely survivable if you have warm clothes. However at this elevation the terrain isn't very flat in any given direction and, in the poor visibility that accompanies bad weather, you stand a good chance of falling off whatever you're on if you wander indiscriminately about.

Secondly there are avalanches. Bad weather usually causes them. When they're happening (you know when they are by the roar they make) it's best to stay put. Of course this means that you're not skiing your trophy line.

Third is time. Sad to say we all must work for a living. There are only so many five day periods one can take off without getting canned, even from such a loose job as writing. Like night follows day, one's infrequent five days off coincide with bad weather and avalanches.

Fourth there are friends. You need them to accompany you on a trophy line hunt. Primarily they serve to dig you out of an avalanche if you get buried. They also serve as good companions when you're stormbound in your tent. They also get sick, fatigued, and mentally weary of the whole business of bagging a trophy line and insist on going home.

This is to be expected. One expects that even oneself, arch trophy line hunter that one is, will get sick, fatigued, and weary of such a soul-shaking pastime. After all, we're talking about going out in the middle of winter when sane folks are sipping toddies by the fire. But, in the end, there's the map on the wall and that beautiful sinuous line of valleys, passes, high ridges, and peaks that clamor to be skied in one clean, pure, uninterrupted go. Yes, the trophy line rears its magnificent head again.

Well, I went in December, in January, February, March, and April. I went with girlfriends, with mountaineering friends, with good friends and so-so friends. We tried at the full moon, at the waning moon, at no moon. We tried when the weatherman said it couldn't possibly snow. And it snowed like the next ice age was coming. We tried leaving in the thick of blizzards, hoping by our devious counter measures, to trick the weather into letting up. It never did. And when it wasn't snowing it was abominably cold, and the cold kept the snowpack unstable and avalanche prone. When it wasn't snowing or cold and everything was absolutely perfect, I got sick. Or my friends got sick. Sometimes we got sick simultaneously. And sometimes we got scared, which is maybe why we said we were sick. After all, a person can get eaten by a trophy line – even when the moment seems perfect for the dash, it's hard to force yourself to ski out into all that empty whiteness. But I guess such falterings of the heart eventually give you a sense of accomplishment if you finally make the go.

As I said, we tried six times to bring down a trophy line (winter lasts a long time in these parts) and when May finally rolled around we became certain that we were going to bag it – not by skill, oh no, but by tiredness . . . its own. You see, like a great stag that has expended himself in bugling, fighting, and rutting, the winter runs down come May. The endless Pacific fronts begin to break up, the weather turns mild and sunny, and the sun, now high and smiling in the sky, melts the snow. It takes a long time for twenty feet of mountain snow to melt. In fact it takes until August. In May and June, though, the consolidation that takes place produces a very special kind of snowpack. Individual winter crystals collapse together in a lubricated fraternity and at night freeze. Called "corn," this frozen surface is ideal for skiing. You can bag the steepest day tour line without fear of it avalanching, and you can travel anywhere through the mountains without breaking trail. The truth is you can sneak up on a sleeping trophy line and without the least bit of trouble bop it over the head. Okay, it's not exactly how the alpine heroes might do it, but as I said, we tried six times in winter conditions and failed.

Our line, however, had other plans. It snowed in April and it snowed in May. And when we thought it had to stop snowing, it snowed some more. By mid May when, in a usual year, day tour and trophy lines are lying everywhere belly up for the taking, the mountains were still grumbling and spitting. A giant slide came off Mt. Axtel and shot spruce trees a foot in diameter onto the

Kebler Pass road amid a hail of green confetti. Baldy Mountain, pretty close to our trophy line, let out a slab avalanche – the kind most always seen in winter – whose fracture line could be seen from town by nearsighted people. Spooky. Then the pilot who was going to pick us up at the end of our trophy line told us that he'd seen half of the Maroon Bells slide onto Buckskin Pass – one of those particularly adventurous passages we had planned.

Martyrdom is such a poetic state when confined to history books. Faced with it in your own backyard, and without the incentive of imperiled country or kin, much less the promise of financial reward, one stays safely at home. At least that's what we did.

As a sop, we skied the Red Lady, a safe, beautiful day tour line that sits above town. Granted, it was like calling up an old girlfriend when your other prospects haven't panned out. But we enjoyed it and I'm sure The Lady was happy having the old crew up for a morning. Even so, we didn't ski her bowl. Dubious about her steepest side, we chose her gentler southwest shoulder and were back at home, eating flapjacks and listening to an inspirational concert come over the cable from Chicago, by 10:30 in the morning: Safe, civil and somewhat unsatisfying, especially when you consider that from the summit of Red Lady we could see the country to the north – Paradise Divide, Fravert Basin, Snowmass Mountain – still tempting us.

A week went by. The sun came out in earnest. I asked friends, "Hey, want to do the trophy line?" The looked at me as if they weren't quite sure what they'd heard. You must realize that the first pansies had come out and the aspen had begun to bloom. "The snow's all corned up," I added enthusiastically, "it'll take just a few days."

"You're mad," said one insensitive person.

"Let's go boating," said another.

What was I to do? I donned my skis and glided up the valley of Oh-Be-Joyful alone. I camped in a meadow, in the moonlight, and listened to three coyotes sing before clouds covered the moon and two inches of snow fell.

In the morning I broke camp early. Aiming for the high pass four miles away, I began to ski up Oh-Be-Joyful Creek, its water muted beneath several feet of sagging snow. I guess I felt joyful, but not completely. On each side of the valley 2000-foot slopes, cut by maroon cliffs, rose to the sky. Lots of snow perched up there, lots.

A coyote track crossed my path. I stopped. Now, in addition to a trophy line providing day tour lines along the way, it occasionally presents the skier with different sorts of educational and general-interest lines that lie ripe for exploration. This is why you often take an extra day's food on a trophy line hunt – to give you time to poke around. Well, I wanted to get up to the pass before the snow softened too much and became prone to sliding. But I also wanted to see what the coyote was up to. I was sure that it must have been one of the trio that sang me to sleep. Curiosity won over ambition.

I followed the track south and found the coyote's bed in some willows that had caught first sun. Backtracking, I skied along the paw prints and crossed the creek, went into the spruce forest, crawled under some blowdowns, and came back onto the northern slopes of the valley. The coyote, nosing here and there among the tree moats, was hunting snowshoe hares, whose prints lay everywhere like stadium litter after a football game. From tree to tree, widely scattered across the slope, the coyote sniffed. At one point her pawprints (I had decided, by the size of the tracks and their daintiness, that the coyote was a female) went straight up a 60-degree wall of snow, bounding for 50 feet before reaching a bench. I went around the steep wall and found her tracks on the bench. They continued into the forest.

Up, up, the coyote climbed. Hating her relentlessness, wanting to get back on route, torn between bagging the trophy line and just for once following a chanced-upon track to its conclusion, I let the coyote lead me. Here, on the cold, shady, north side of the valley, the crust was frozen under the trees and not much new snow had fallen through the dense boughs. Trailing was difficult, but I always found her prints emerging from a tree moat. As far as I could tell, she never met a hare. I had to sidestep in places, for the ground was too steep for the skins of my skis to hold.

Finally we neared treeline. Her prints went into a tree well, down I followed, and when I slid out the other side her prints were nowhere to be seen. I made a half circle around the moat; nothing. I went back to the far side of the depression. Sure enough, her prints hunted directly toward the trunk, faded on the crust, and vanished. Impossible! Just to make sure, I looked up the tree. She wasn't there. Then I skied wider and wider circles around the moat, having to sidestep up the steep forested tiers above. At last I found new snow. But the coyote's tracks had been removed as effectively as if she had sprouted wings.

Feeling misled by the coyote, I stopped and leaned on my poles and stared up valley toward my pass. As I watched, an avalanche slid away and covered the entire route I would have taken.

I skied back to town and waited a few days for the backcountry to truly settle down. In the first week of June (June, mind you!) everything seemed poised for one final attempt. I had even found another dedicated trophy line hunter to go along, though rumor has it that I bribed her.

We loaded our packs, we skinned up our skis, we stepped out the mudroom of the house (pretty well filled with mud), and where dark clouds had been building on Paradise Divide a serpent's tongue of lightning flicked down, touched the white peaks, and sent a roll of thunder booming down the valley.

A wind followed, the trees heeled over toward the swollen creek and, as we stood with our skis on our shoulders, the gray sky opened with warm, shining drops of rain. We shuffled back into the house and let the winter, a bear I had harried too long, fall asleep in its den.

The Straight Edge

WHY a few of our tools are regularly introduced by the definite article is a question worth discussing. For instance one learns *the* fly rod, trains on *the* bike and shaves with *the* straight edge. Perhaps the reason for this usage has to do with respect for quiet power. You see, in the hands of the accomplished a flyrod cast into the wind, or a lightweight cycle heeled around a corner, become objects of grace. But put that rod or bike into the hands of the clumsy, or that most wretched of individuals, the beginner who thinks he knows a thing or two, and they'll frustrate and even harm their wielder. I know. My apprenticeship of the rod and bike began years ago – in childhood.

The straight edge, however, I didn't pick up until well after puberty. You might even say that I was an adult. Naturally, I didn't wake up one morning and say, "Today I am going to shave with the straight edge." No, my schooling with this tool began circuitously – by fits and starts and by what, at the time, seemed innocent enough meanderings. In fact, I probably never would have picked up the razor if I hadn't shaved off my beard, and I probably would never have shaved it off if I hadn't married. The first followed close upon the heels of the second.

My wife and I had moved from Crested Butte, a small town in the Colorado Rockies, to Boulder, a university town located in the foothills north of Denver. Joyce, a ballet teacher, wanted to study dance under a new teacher, (ballet, by the way, is often called, with double italics, *The Dance*), and I, thinking that I really didn't know much about writing, wanted to go to grad school which, at least in English, is never called *the* grad school.

In the big city we had little need for the snowboots, down parks, and wool knickers that had been our daily clothing in Crested Butte. Joyce, feeling her instinctual buying urges warmed by the many shop windows, outfitted us in what she called "our uptown look" – dresses, trousers, and sportcoats. Unfortunately, my full beard didn't go with this new look. After a month of cajoling from Joyce (who at five-foot-seven and 101 pounds is as far from a lumberjack's woman as can be imagined), I shaved it off and was surprised to see the person who appeared. The stranger looked ten years younger, ten pounds thinner, and infinitely less demonic and mountain-crazed. Yet the lost decade didn't bring back the pudgy undergraduate I remembered. On the contrary, the face that emerged from the suds had a skeptically humorous, sideways, and ironic smile, as if I had somehow developed the habit of drinking expensive bottles of wine while hearing of my pending economic ruin. Joyce loved the change.

So did I. But, to tell the truth, I had no affection for how the transformation had been wrought. My Gillette TRAC II razor had no weight in the hand, seemingly no value lying by the tap, and, to make matters worse, left a weekly litter of *disposable* cartridges. (This is when Joyce and I faithfully separated our trash into compost, aluminum, paper, glass and plastic.) Shaving with this bit of techno-whiz was highly functional but somehow soulless – like living in a city to get an education, like moving into a townhouse because we didn't have enough time to renovate an old home with more character, like making love to your wife and simultaneously thinking of the woman whom you had seen in the English office when you had gone to register for next semester's classes.

Sigh.

Returning the can of Gillette Foamy to the medicine cabinet, I avoided my eyes. Had I done that? I had, hadn't I? Yes, I had. And I still had enough remaining catechism to feel guilty. How could I be sniffing along the coed trail when everyone – my friends, my parents, the secretary of the department – said, "Oh, you have such a beautiful wife." Indeed, I had to agree. She was beautiful – amber-eyed, tawny, lean from dancing, skiing, and chopping wood, the mountain air still lighting her hair and flushing under her cheeks. But that flush was disappearing in her, and in me, and to everyone who envied her thinness saying, "Oh, to have a metabolism like hers," I wanted to reply, "My friend, that's not metabolism. That's eating nothing but alfalfa sprouts and Perrier. And sometimes, when she's feeling fat because she hasn't skied or hiked in addition to having danced, she'll puke up dinner just to make sure."

The fat, for Joyce, had become *the* urban battle, one she fought with heavy artillery – 100 situps per day, 200 plies, 500 battements – until the skin on her belly wouldn't have made a mouthful for a starving rat. Then her menses went and, slowly, her desire.

Double sigh.

Seeing as she had been happier and healthier – okay, why beat around the bush, not an anorexic – in the mountains, I thought that maybe the mountains might let her walk hard, climb high, and eat lots. I had time before the semester started; she was not thrilled with the people who taught her dance classes. And we had some money saved.

We flew to India, took a train to the border of Nepal and a truck to Kathmandu. For the next two months we roamed around the eastern Himalaya, eating rice, noodles, and potatoes, taking in our belts once a week, and climbing five peaks. We had English names for things – the passes, mountains, and high pastures – and Nepali names for these same places and also Tibetan words. And then we had our own special names, sounds we made in our throats and the looks we shared, which no one else could understand. We never felt healthier, or freer. But it couldn't last. From the summit of the last peak we climbed – as we looked over the ridge of Everest and into the yellow steppes of Tibet, the sky blue as the eyes of Buddha, watching over Shiva and his consort Kali – my Kali leaned against me and said, "Theo, I want to go home. I need to dance." She began to cry and I put my arms around her.

"Stay if you want," she said.

"I couldn't do that."

"You know what, Theo. You should have married one of your Outward Bound ladies. Then you would have been happy."

I thought about that and knew she had hit the mark. She would never love the mountains as I did. But she had forgotten one important thing. "They couldn't dance," I said.

We trekked back to Kathmandu and flew home. I started school and also began to run. Hard. Very hard. Every day. Sixty miles a week. Sixty-five miles a week. Two-hundred-fifty miles a month. What else can you do in a city?

Dance, *naturallment*. Joyce began to rehearse "Swan Lake," stayed late at the studio and worked in a pub while I found additional and not always creative writing assignments. One has to pay the rent somehow. And because of our jobs and because we each trained for the dance and for the run, we often ate at times designed to maximize our performance. So often we ate alone. Once, after elk season, a friend from Crested Butte sent us some venison and, thinking to surprise her, I sautéed it, and also made some brocolli, rice, and muffins because I doubted she would eat deer. She walked in, her nose crinkled, and she said "meat" the way Quakers say sin.

"I cooked you some rice and vegetables."

"The smell makes me ill."

I stared at the skillet after she went downstairs, thinking of how she had once, at least, eaten trout. I could hear her doing battements in the bedroom.

I left the meal on the stove, went upstairs to where I wrote. On the desk there was a pile of books and a clipboard holding blank typing paper. I sat down and drew a little infinity sign on the paper. The curves of the shape have always made me feel good.

After a while she also came upstairs, padded across the carpet and put her arms around me. She said, "I'm sorry, Theo." I turned around and put my legs around her.

She touched my face. "I'm glad you took your beard off when we came home." I pulled at my bare chin. It was a few weeks before Christmas – that time when you're either humming carols or thinking that the 23 degree tilt of the earth's axis, creating this dark corner of the year, is one of the worst jokes the cosmos ever played. "J.," I said, "I want a straight edge."

"Straight edge?"

"Razor. You know. Shh-shh." I made a stropping motion.

"Suicide or murder?"

"Excitement."

"A straight edge, huh?"

"Yep, a straight edge."

On Noel morn the asked-for item, along with a leather strop, a badger brush, shaving mug, and properly scented, masculine soap appeared under the tree. The razor had a black handle and a dapper blade. On the neck of the blade was inscribed the name Hoffritz and beneath it, with great restraint, Germany.

My parents had come out for the holiday and my Dad, a Gillette safety man from his teens, cast a suspicious eye at the razor. He picked it up as if fingering a stick of dynamite, turned to Joyce, and said, in a tone of voice that indicated she might be the cause of his not having grandchildren, "Knew a fella who slit his throat with one of those."

Fortunately, I had shaved before coming down to the tree and so everyone was spared my untimely death on the holiday. The next day Joyce and I had a morning visit and so, once again, I didn't have the time to explore the straight edge. Christmas week being what it is, my postponement of learning the straight edge continued. I could hardly forget it, though, sitting as it was by the sink like a loaded gun.

Always one for receiving proper instruction in the use of deadly tools, I went, shortly after New Year's, to a local barber shop. The proprietor, a white-haired gentleman, escorted me to the chair and adjusted the cape and collar. I said, "Could you please give me a shave?"

His face took on a look of anxiety. I might have told him that Uncle Sam had defaulted on one of his T-Bills.

"Come again," he said.

"I want a shave. With the straight edge over there." I pointed to the razor standing in its jar of blue liquid.

The barber laughed nervously, bent close, and said, "I haven't shaved anyone in years."

"Could you give it a try?"

He did. But he was so tentative, so unsure, so unwilling to commit the blade to my face that I left nearly as bewhiskered as I had entered. I learned nothing.

A few more days went by. Each morning I rose, brushed my teeth, and my hand, straying toward the straight edge . . . found the Gillette. Joyce, who had spent no small sum on my Christmas infatuation, asked, "When are you going to shave with it?"

"Soon," I said. "Give me time."

On Saturday, when she was at her morning dance class, I brewed a strong pot of coffee, took a steaming cup to the bathroom, and began to soak my face in hot towels as I had seen barbers do in the movies. With the towels wrapped around my face, I stropped the razor. The soft noise of steel on cowskin was soothing. I half closed my eyes and listened – almost the whisper of skis through snow – and stroked quicker, surer. When I ran the blade over my fingernail it removed a curl. Okay. Ready.

I took a sip of coffee. I picked up the brush. I soaked it under the tap, swirled it on the sandlewood soap, and painted cauliflowers of lather on my cheeks and neck. When done, I winked at myself in the mirror and gave my best here-we-go smile. Without hesitating, I lifted the razor and quickly scraped it across my cheek. It made the sound of sandpaper on wood. I winced and tried again. Again the sanding noise and a stubborn tugging. Not to be put off, I worked upward, toward my sideburn, noting that the suds had begun to turn red.

Wondering what I might be doing wrong, I leaned close to the mirror and rested the razor on my upper lip in a reflective pose. A ruby line spit around the blade. Sticking tissue on my mouth, I proceeded to my neck. Up under the chin – whoosh, swish – pull back the skin with the fingers, smoothly stretch the jowels ahead of the blade, nothing to it at all. As in all sports, one needs to warm up. Blood began to drip down my chest.

Just then Joyce came home. I heard her put down her grocery

bags and come upstairs. Why hide one's clumsiness? I turned around.

"Ugh!" It was the noise she made when we passed an auto accident. She went to the telephone and began to leaf through the yellow pages.

"I don't need a doctor," I said. Blood spattered the carpet.

Always one to treat the cause and not the symptoms, she glanced at me and said, "I was looking for barber schools."

There was one in Denver, but I never attended. I felt that learning the straight edge was the sort of thing you perfected at the knee of a mentor – some profound and unlikely mixture of Rudyard Kipling's father and the barber who shaved Wyatt Earp in Tombstone. I, however, found Fred, the Mexican owner of the barber shop near campus. He had thick, laborer's hands, and, as I watched him through his shopwindow, he moved them quickly over his customer's face and left no blood. The next day I brought him my Hoffritz.

"What's wrong?" I said.

He touched the blade with his thumb and said, "Needs honing." He laid the blade on a stone and stroked from its toe to its heel many times. Then he brought it close to his eye, blew on it, and handed it back. "If I was you," he said, "I'd get a safety razor. It's quicker."

Didn't mentors always throw such curve balls at their students? I took up Fred's challenge. Faithfully, I honed my razor each morning and continued to strop it. Now having a blade with a much finer edge, I was, of course, able to cut myself with greater dexterity. At the few faculty parties we went to, Joyce said, "Oh, my husband? He's learning the straight edge." When I passed my undergraduate students on campus, I overheard them say, "Oh, no. He's learning the straight edge." And at the used bookstore near campus, the owner, who had always worn a scholarly Van Dyke, appeared sheepishly one day from behind his stacks. He was smooth-shaven, though scarred about his chin with tiny scabs. I looked at him. He looked at me. "The straight edge?" he said.

I nodded.

"I should have kept my beard."

"Less wind resistance," I consoled. "It's better for running."

"Too athletic." He reached for his pipe and added, "I smoke."

I shrugged, I smoked too – small black cigars – while sitting over Propertius, Bartes, or the nonsense I wrote myself. This habit, which was trés chic in the local cafes, seemed perfectly stupid, considering that I was also running intervals at the track to increase my speed. But silly as it seemed, it kept something in my mouth, and that proved comforting.

This was the time I hardly ever saw Joyce, who, as long as we're being truthful, hardly ever saw me. She had her rehearsals and I had my writing and we had a system that I have heard other writers have used. Joyce came home and called up the stairs, "Can I talk to you?" If I was in the midst of being unfaithful and embracing the lady muse, I'd call back, "No."

"Will you eat dinner?"

"Maybe."

Inevitably, eight became nine, ten, and then eleven o'clock, and Joyce, exhausted from a day at the studio was almost always sleeping when I came to bed. If she wasn't we'd talk about our day – what she had danced and what I had written, how the run had gone and, if we were still awake, she'd ask me what I had had for dinner and I'd say, "Oh, pasta. What'd you have?" And she'd say, "Oh, it was too late, so I just had a glass of wheatgrass juice."

Her back was curled into my chest, my arms around her. Then she might say, talking low like she was falling asleep but with an excited burble in her throat that made her voice go husky, how fruitarianism was the logical antecedent to breatharianism (that is, living so purely one need only breathe air). She was well on the road to it. The day before, while pulling on her leotard, she had said, "Ninety-eight pounds, Theo. At last." Then she started telling me how wheatgrass juice had killed her appetite and how four ounces of the green stuff contained all the vitamins, proteins, and carbohydrates anyone needed for a whole day. I put my face in her hair. I had had an English muffin before coming to bed and felt like the Cyclops ripping the heads off Ulysses' men.

"When you're writing and running hard, Theo," she asked sleepily, "doesn't your desire go way down?"

"No," I said. "It doesn't."

"It must be diet," she said. "Mine does." And she rolled away from me.

I lay there, my palm still on her back. She lay there, lying there. Then I heard her breathing become slower and she slept.

I actually got good at the straight edge after that. I got so good I could go one day without cutting myself badly. And my face hardly looked raw anymore, though it stayed tender around the jowels, which for me have always been hard to shave.

One afternoon, while I sat at my desk and read Catallus, the phone rang. It was a friend at a trekking agency in Seattle and she told me that Cho Oyu, a very high and beautiful mountain on the Nepalese-Tibetan border, which Joyce and I had hiked beneath, had been opened to foreign expeditions. Years before, some other climbers and I had applied to climb it and had been turned down by the Nepalese government. My friend at the trekking agency said, "I don't have to tell you how many people will be applying. Get in your permit ASAP."

I stubbed out the cigar I had been smoking and called everyone I could find who had been on the original permit. By dinner four of us had maps and photos spread on my livingroom floor, lists of equipment made and the tasks divided. After my friends had left, I sat in the middle of the happy mess and reviewed the application we had written. Joyce came in. She looked tired. She had been at the studio eight hours.

"J.," I said. "Cho Oyu is open."

She slumped in the chair by the window and didn't take off her coat. She looked at me hard and said, "When are we going to have a baby?"

This seemed a frivolous question on her part. But I said, "After graduate school. Next year. We can have a baby anytime, and I can go to Cho Oyu. It's only a couple months."

She looked at me even harder. "Theo," she said. "There'll always be another Cho Oyu for you."

She took off her coat, went to the kitchen, fixed herself a salad, and went downstairs to our bedroom.

That spring she spent three weeks in New York, dancing. She came back as thin, and as beautiful, as she had ever been. We packed some food and gear and drove to the Wind River Mountains in Wyoming, where we had spent our honeymoon. But that had been Augusts ago and now it was June and we found six feet of snow. Not to worry. Weren't we two old mountain folks? We went in on snowshoes, carrying 80-pound packs, and fell through the rotten spring snow at every step. After the first mile, Joyce threw her pack down and sat on it. "I am not a pack mule," she cried. "I'm a dancer."

"Let's go back to Boulder then."

"Urrr," she growled and put on her pack.

We climbed for three weeks and a smarter man would have been happy. But she had had her New York visit and I wanted my rights. Wasn't our marriage one of rights, right down to the red line in the checkbook that balanced our separate finances each month? I did ask her, though, to come to Peru, just as she had asked me to come to New York. And the way I had begged off, saying I had writing that needed to be finished, she begged off, saying that three weeks in the Wind Rivers was enough mountains for one year. She wanted to dance.

We stretched out our Wyoming trip by driving nowhere into Idaho and feeling sad, as if our life had been planned by a bumbling travel agent who had given us too much and not enough time. Our little roadside camping excursion, after the real climbing had been done, caused us to get home on the eve of my departure for South America. I packed in a rush and by midnight we were both so tired that we fell asleep in each other's arms without making love. I had a four AM flight and didn't have time to shave, so I kept the beard I had started in the Wind Rivers.

In the doorway, as I left for Lima, she said, "Come back."

I hugged her and turned around at the bottom of the steps. She wore a filmy nightgown and, with the hall light behind her, seemed naked and clothed by incandescence.

"I will," I said. "I will come back." I wanted to. I wanted to more than anything else in the world. On her point shoes, white and defying gravity, she danced what I would never climb and maybe never write. And she was my wife and so far had put up with me as no one else had. Twenty-four hours later I saw the Southern Cross come up over Lima.

Frank and I were the oldest of friends. We had survived an avalanche; we had loved the same girl; we were Eskimo brothers. On Kitaraju, talking too much, we let the time slip by and crested the summit ridge as the sun went down. The ridge had cornices on both sides and the wind blew snow up around our knees until we couldn't tell where the cornices ended and space began. On one side it was 6000 feet to the valley floor. On the other three. We didn't have many options. Descending the ridge seemed risky. Rapelling back down the north face, which we had climbed, seemed impossible – or at least not much fun in the dark. Bivouacing on the ridge, in a forty mile an hour wind, in below zero temperatures – well, no one had to outline what that would mean. We stood there, the rope coiled in our hands, and when I looked at Frank he had a smile on his face. I guess we'll never know if he was smiling at my smile or the other way around, which is, I guess, why you call someone your Eskimo brother. We turned on our headlamps and started down the ridge, stopping when the wind let up, going carefully, until we found a hole – the opening of a crevasse. It led forty feet down into the ridge and we climbed into it, staying as far as possible from the side that opened into the cornice. At the bottom we sat on our packs. We had no sleeping bags, but that mattered little. We were out of the wind. We rubbed each other's hands and feet and sometimes we dozed, and as I dozed I thought of Joyce going to her ballet class and stopping at the grocery, perhaps going out to do a rock climb – she had said she was going to do more climbing. Soon I'd be home and we could climb together on warm rock, in shorts and T-shirts, drinking a beer afterwards. There had been so many things wrong between us, so many. I could have given her more support, financial and emotional. I could have continued the dance classes I had taken with her on and off, more off than on. I could have agreed to buy the house she had wanted to renovate. I could have done all those things instead of being in this crevasse with Frank. But sitting there, I felt her thinking of me and I said, "I'm coming home, Joyce, and it will be different."

Frank and I got off Kitaraju with all our fingers and toes, and in Huaraz, where we resupplied, I received a letter from Joyce. It said she had been dancing every day and also climbing. It ended with "I love you, I love you, I love you," which sounded too fierce for comfort. I thought of going home right away. Sitting in the courtyard of our hotel, I thought about it for two days while Frank waited and I looked across the pine trees to Huascaran, the tallest peak in the range. It would only take ten days to climb it, which is a short time when stacked up against a lifetime with someone. And Frank, after our bivouac on Kitaraju, was now an even older friend, and Huascaran, she was white as a swan.

In the icefall we lost a day when an Italian climber stumbled into a crevasse and we helped to evacuate him. As we lowered him over the last seracs he died and we lost another day, sitting around camp and thinking about how young he had been and how young we still were. Then we climbed back through the icefall, bivouaced under a bergschrund, and led out two hard pitches the next freezing morning. The hard part was done. We had only a couple thousand feet of easy ground to the summit. We started upwards and a connection that had been coming over the horizon stopped. I stared at the sky through my goggles then looked down to the snow, because that was really the straightest line to Joyce, down through the earth and out to Colorado. But there was no voice and no eyes there either. I climbed a little farther, Frank coming along on the rope behind me. But someone had opened a tap in the sole of my boots and all I had felt about the mountains and me and the woman whom I had thought was mine slipped out into my crampon tracks. I was altitude sick. I sat down and Frank came up.

"I feel terrible," I said.

We went on a bit more, but it was no use. I kneeled down and barfed out my guts, trying to get rid of the illness I felt coming over the horizon.

In Huaraz I tried to call her. She wasn't home, although she should have been. Walking back through town, I looked at myself in the storeglass. My burnt nose and summer's beard made me look old and when I passed Sr. Moreno's barber shop I went in. It was Frank's recommendation.

Sr. Moreno, a round-faced, kind man, lounged in one of his red leather chairs, his feet on the marble counter before him. He jumped up.

"*Buenos tardes*, Don Teodoro." He wrung my hand. "Is Don Francisco alright?"

"Of course."

"Thank God." He tssked his tongue. "You people frighten me. One day I'm shaving you, the next I hear that you've fallen into some crevasse. As if life weren't short enough. Did you hear about the Italian?"

"We carried him down."

"Terrible. His poor wife."

"How about a shave, Sr. Moreno?"

"At last. I knew Don Francisco would convince you. Let's see who you are under there."

He unfurled a towel across my chest and without using hot cloths, or even hot soap, began to shave me. After clearcutting a swath of beard he rubbed his stubby soft fingers over my chin, against the grain, and restroked the blade where he had left some stubble.

"How do you get it so smooth?" I asked.

"Oh, Don Teodoro, many years of practice. But all you have to do is stroke from the toe to the heel of the blade and lift the skin ahead of it."

He told me nothing new. I closed my eyes, heard him lay down the razor and pick up a bottle. A puff of moist air made me leap from the chair. Clutching an atomizer in one hand, he held me down with the other and continued to spray my sunburned cheeks. "Don't worry," he said in a sincere voice, "the alcohol cauterizes everything." After wiping the tears from my eyes with his ever-present towel, he stood back and admired his work. "There," he said. "You will be beautiful for your senora."

She wasn't there. Oh, she picked me up at the airport and we ate dinner together. And even made love. But she wasn't there.

The next day, after her ballet class, we drove up Flagstaff Mountain to boulder on the crags, and at a place where a pine tree grew horizontally out of the rock, she stepped lightly onto the trunk and held a branch as if she were about to faint.

"I . . ." She took a breath. "I met someone else I've been climbing with."

We talked about this man – whom I knew and whom she had known and whom we had both climbed with together – for about an hour, at which point she said, "I think he's my twin." Then we talked two days more – over meals, in bed, and in bars – having one of those discussions that is not negotiation but an attempt to expatiate guilt and patch up a broken ego. Of course, no words can do what a touch would have healed.

She moved out, got her own apartment, and my first night in the half-empty house I felt like a man who has survived a major flood – rage that so many tender possessions had been washed away, relief that what I had secretly wanted to be rid of, but hadn't had the courage to relinquish, had also gone out the door.

I slept in my office. I couldn't face our bedroom. The next morning I woke groggily and stared at my unpacked gear in the corner – ice axes, boots, film cannisters. Textbooks lay on the desk along with an unfinished column, which was due in New York at the end of the week. The phone began to ring and I let it ring. It rang twelve times as I looked in the mirror, deciding whether to start a new beard or shave. Wavering, I thought of the British officer who, while being held prisoner by the Japanese in Burma, had shaved every day of World War II because, as he later said, it kept up discipline, both his own and his men's. I ran the hot water, lathered quickly, honed and stropped the blade, then cut my face to ribbons.

She came by while I stood in the garden. She had a yellow flower in her hair and didn't look two years older. The house, rented out to students since I had moved back to the mountains, had needed a facelift before new renters took over. I had come down to Boulder for a few days, put in some junipers and a bed

of phlox, dabbed paint on the hallway, and had left a note at her
studio.

We sat on the front grass. Warm, shady sun fell through the
elms and as always at this time of year, we both wore running
shorts. She asked about Alaska and about what I was climbing,
because climbing was still what attached us. In fact, in the
months after she had moved out that's all we did together –
climb. Sometimes after reaching a belay ledge high above South
Boulder Creek we sat for an hour or two and talked about the
dance, the writing, and the run and how she needed someone
who wouldn't travel so much and how I needed a *campañera*,
another nomad like myself. Sometimes, when she was climbing
with him and would be an hour late to meet me, I wanted to
punch in her beautiful straight nose and came close to doing so,
but did no more than tell her that she was more selfish than I
thought. Then a day or two later, she would call and say she
needed to talk and let's have dinner. And once or twice after
eating we made love, sadly because it really was goodbye, and
with respect for the pride that had broken us and which the other
couldn't change. We did that so much – talking and climbing into
the dusks of that fall, and skiing through the winter during which
we decided to stand before another judge – that two springs later
we had come to the opposite side of the bell curve which has
been merely one small part of the infinity sign carrying her and
me along: first friends and lovers, then man and wife, then lovers
and finally, seasons later, re-emerged friends. Perhaps it would
have been wiser to have skipped everything in between.

Shyly, she said, "I saw a story you did. Theo – " She waited until
I looked up. "It was the best. The best you've ever done."

I bit my lip. Not once when we were married had she said that.

Then she opened her purse and took out some photos of her
last performance. There were several dressing room shots, some
of the chorus, and one of her in a pas de deux. The last showed
her in a jeté that must have been five feet off the stage. She
seemed suspended and wore a smile for the crowd in the back. "A
Lincoln Center jeté," I said. I wanted to say something else but
my voice wouldn't do it. There wasn't a trace in that jeté of the
struggle she had undergone – the bleeding toes, the shinsplints,

her sobs in the bathroom as dinner went down the sink – and what she had really given up . . . the mountains. I wanted to say I'm so proud of you, but my voice wouldn't do it.

"You deserve it," I said. "And you look great." I handed back the photographs. "Hundred seven pounds, I bet. No more Auschwitz face."

"Hundred five." She looked shyly at the grass. "I got my period back."

"No babies yet?"

"Not yet."

Just as shy, and without raising her eyes, she asked, "Did you meet anyone in Alaska?"

"Bears."

She laughed and said, "I've got a class."

We stood up and hugged. She still had one of the most interesting bodies I had ever held – perfect, and hard, as sculpture.

As she gathered her purse she mentioned, "I've got a performance next week, if you're still around."

"Probably not," I said. "You know me. . . . J. – "

She turned; I touched her hand. "You looked wonderful in that photo." I smiled, but I knew my face looked sad. "I'm proud of you."

She looked at my face and sent me a smile back, not small, not large, not as sad as mine, but neither one that I would remember as happy. It was the smile two people share who have been married a long time, married somehow before they met and, somehow, even after they had parted.

The garden took another day to finish and when it was done I retrieved a few kitchen things from the garage – some towels, an orange juice squeezer, and a coffee grinder. I also found a bathrobe I had been searching for and as I lifted it from the trunk the straight edge fell out of its folds. I picked it up, opened the blade, and took a curl off the back of my fingernail. Still sharp. But since the day I had cut my face badly and had gone back to Gillette, I had had two years of faultless shaving – not a knick. I closed the blade and put the straight edge back in the trunk, which I covered with boxes that held books I had once read and photos that had once hung on my walls. I locked the garage and as I got in the car I thought that someday I might use the razor again, if I had a place where I could unpack all my possessions. Such tools need an owner with more than steady hands. He needs the honest heart.

Acknowledgments

This book, built on essays that originally appeared in magazines, or which were drafted while on more newsy assignments, would not have been possible without the generous support of the following people. First and foremost, Tom Paugh of *Sports Afield*, who has not only been a kind editor and friend, but who also has been my magazine father. Jay Cassell, at the same magazine, who has edited my columns for the past six years and many of my manuscripts, I'd also like to thank for his willingness to engage in an editor-writer interchange and his rarely questioning my more harebrained schemes. I'd also like to thank Les Line, Ruth Norris, Gary Soucie and Leslie Ware of *Audubon*, who bought manuscripts over the transom, which no one else would publish, and who have given me some provocative assignments. In addition, the following people have helped in their own special way: Jim Tabor, formerly of *Cross-Country Skier Magazine* and *Backpacker*, who bought pieces that had been rejected at half-a-dozen other magazines; Gaylord Guenin formerly of the old and loved *Mountain Gazette*, which gave a forum to many Rocky Mountain writers; Janet Francendese of Temple University Press and Colgate University, who has given moral support and critique over the past fifteen years; and Judith Schnell at Stackpole who felt that this book was not only worth publishing but would also make money.